I0481324

The Sea Maiden

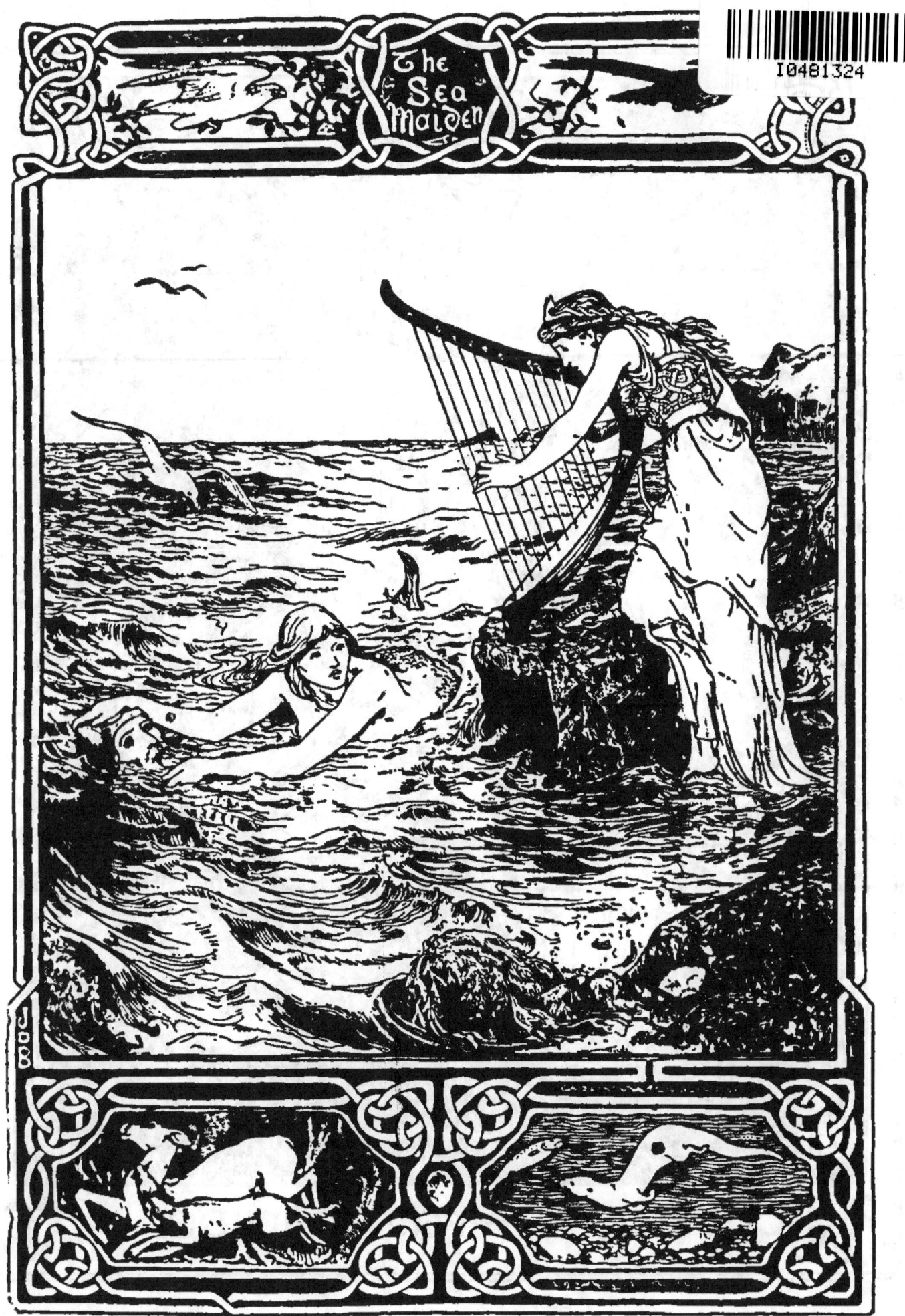

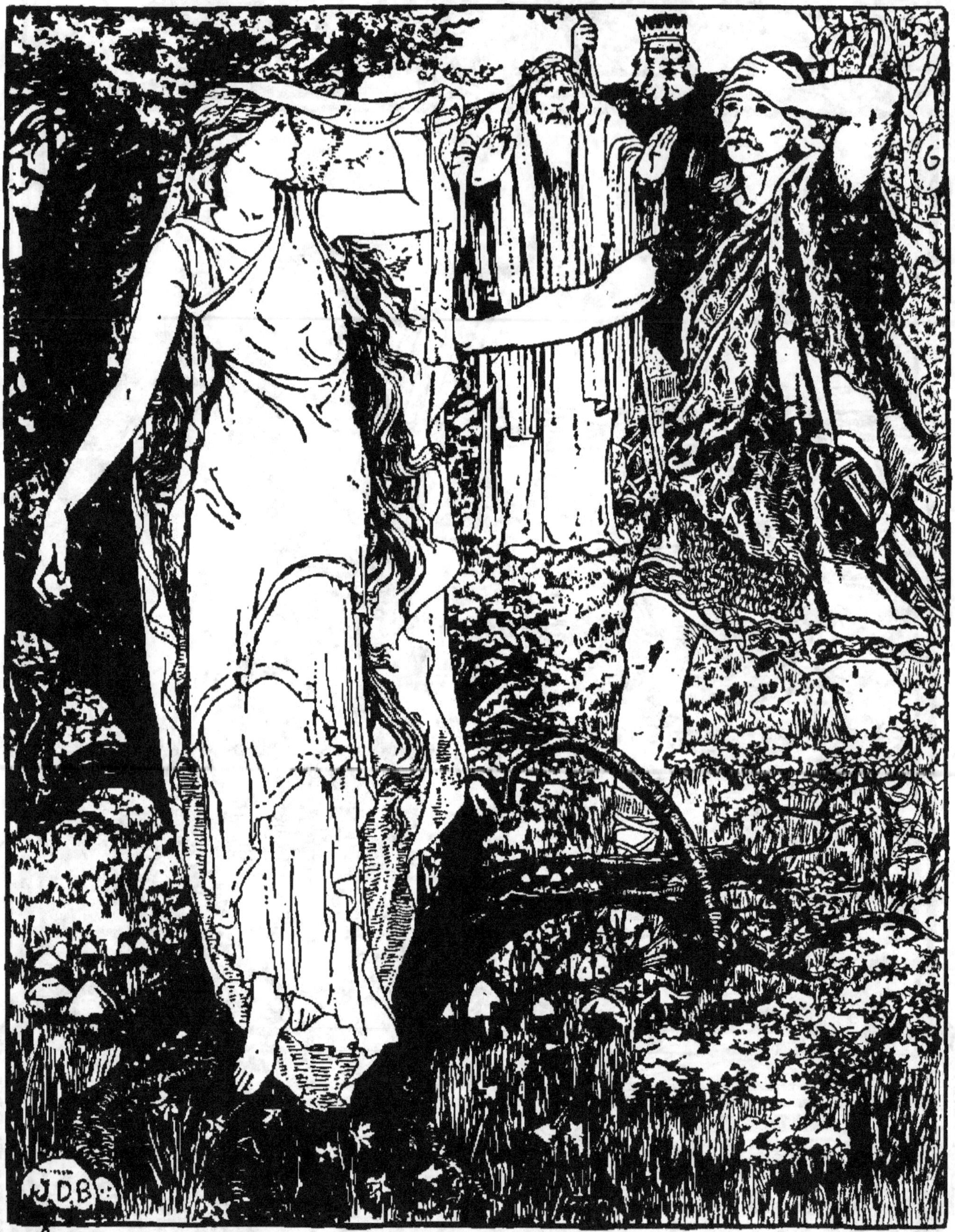

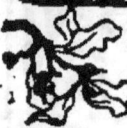
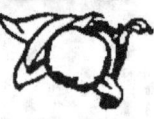

CONNLA and the FAIRY. MAIDEN

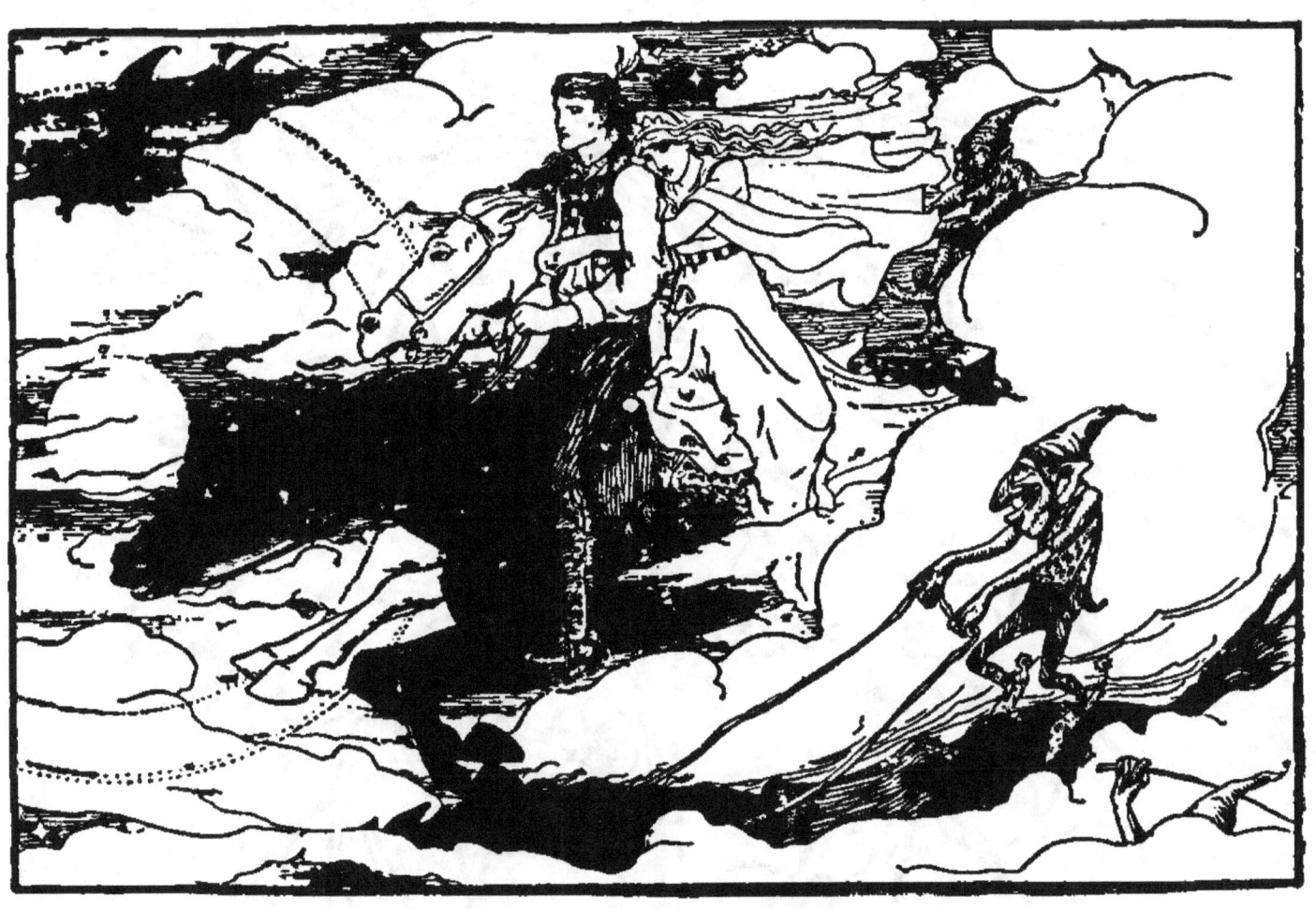

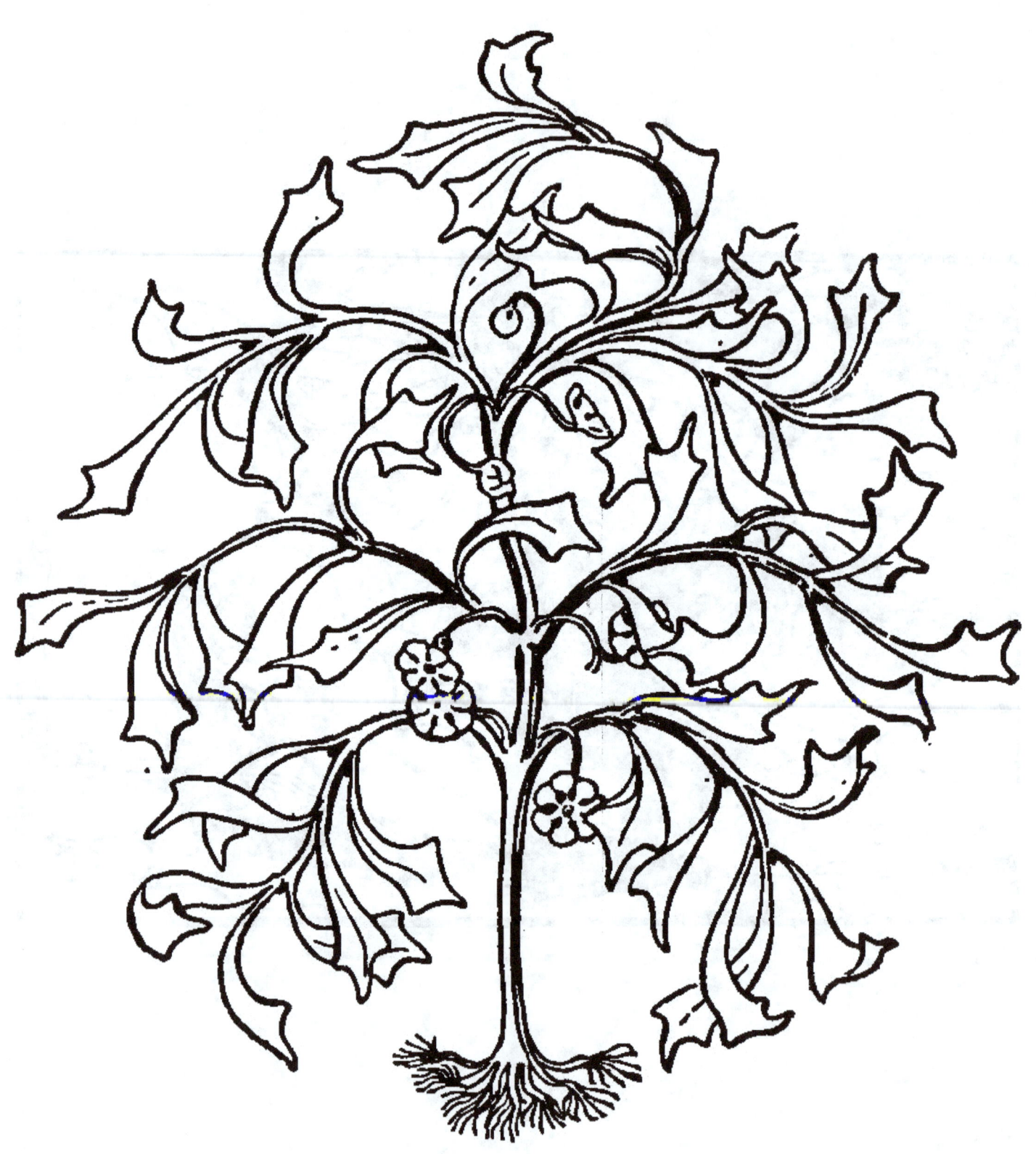

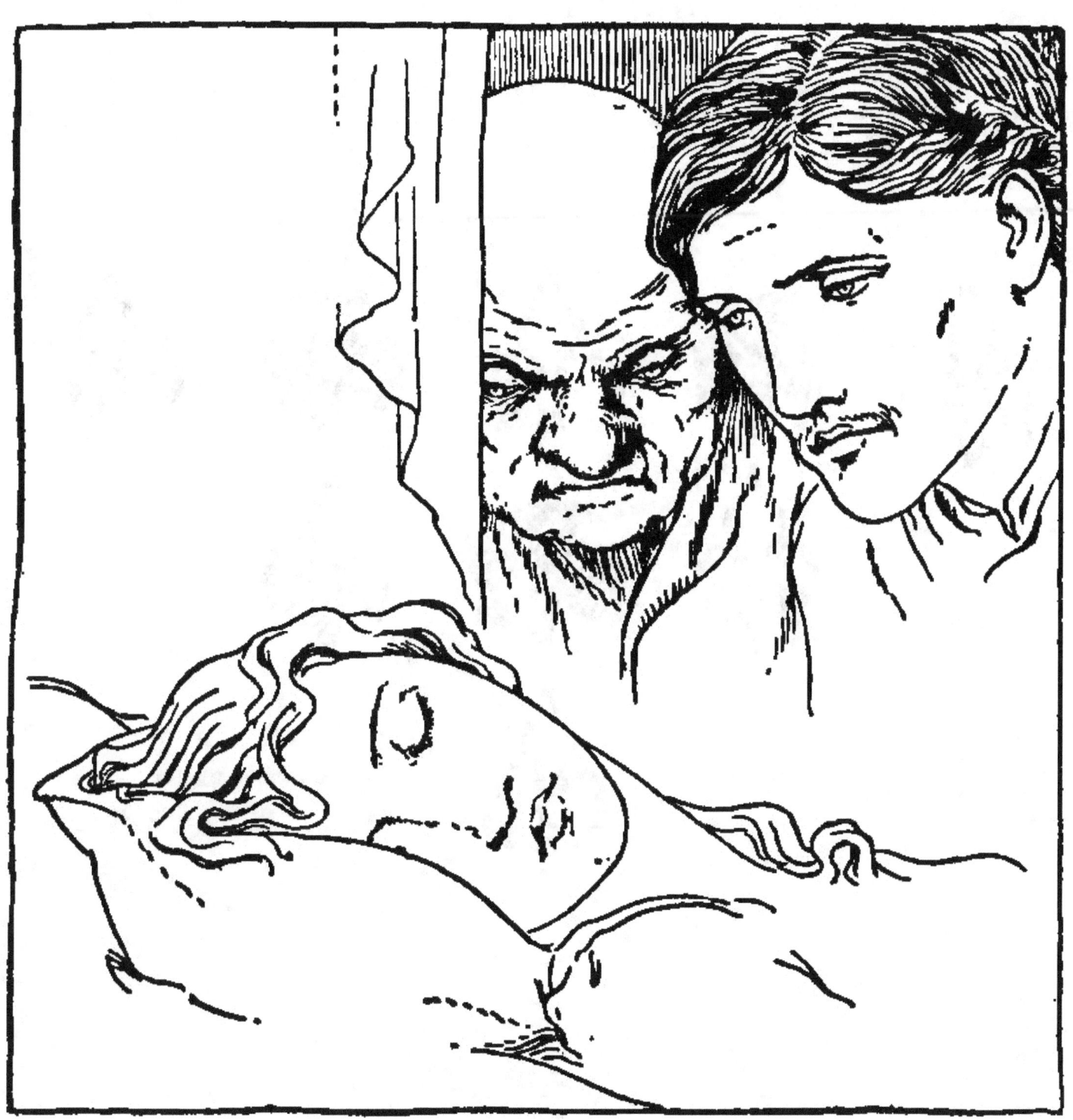

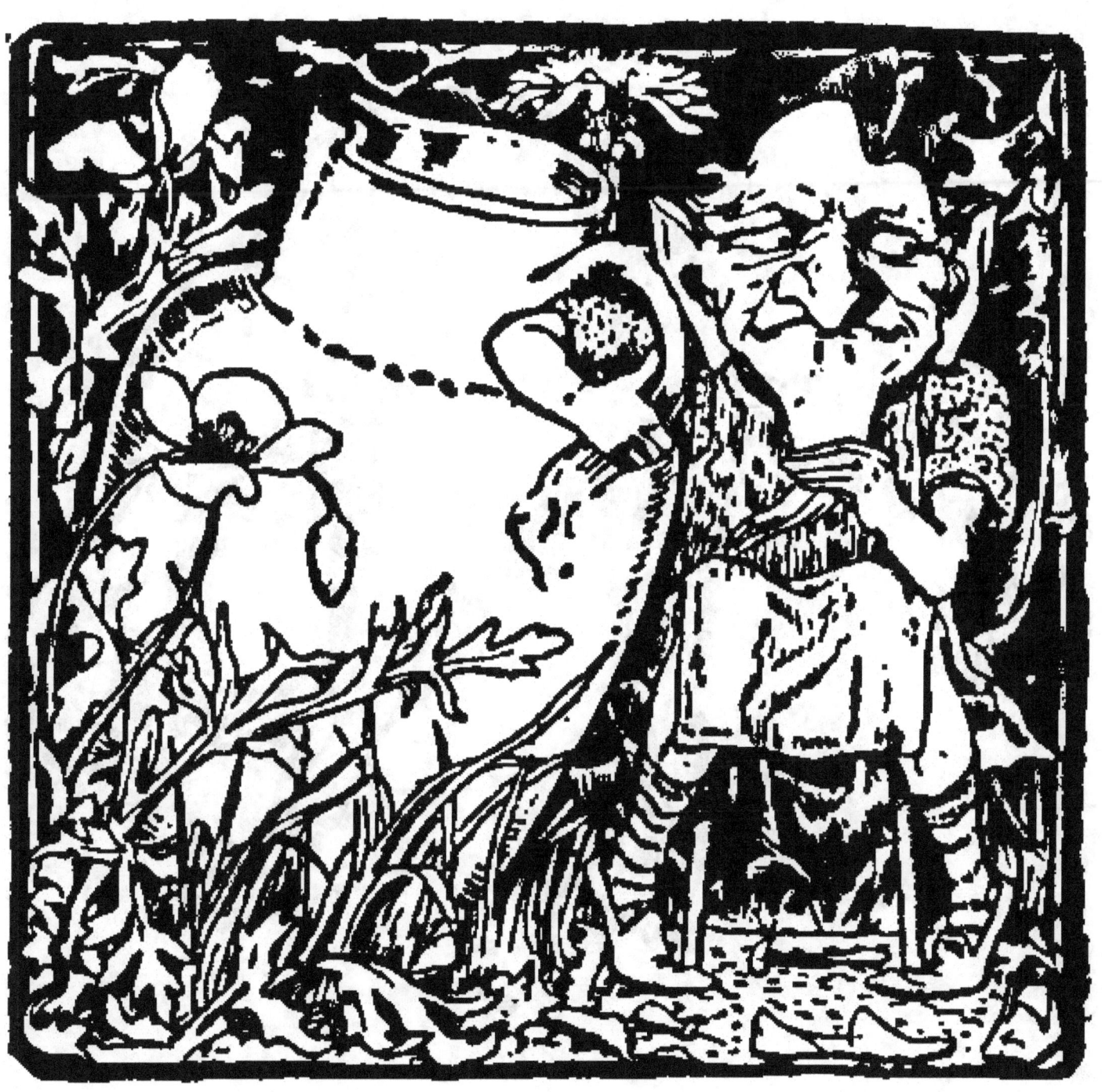

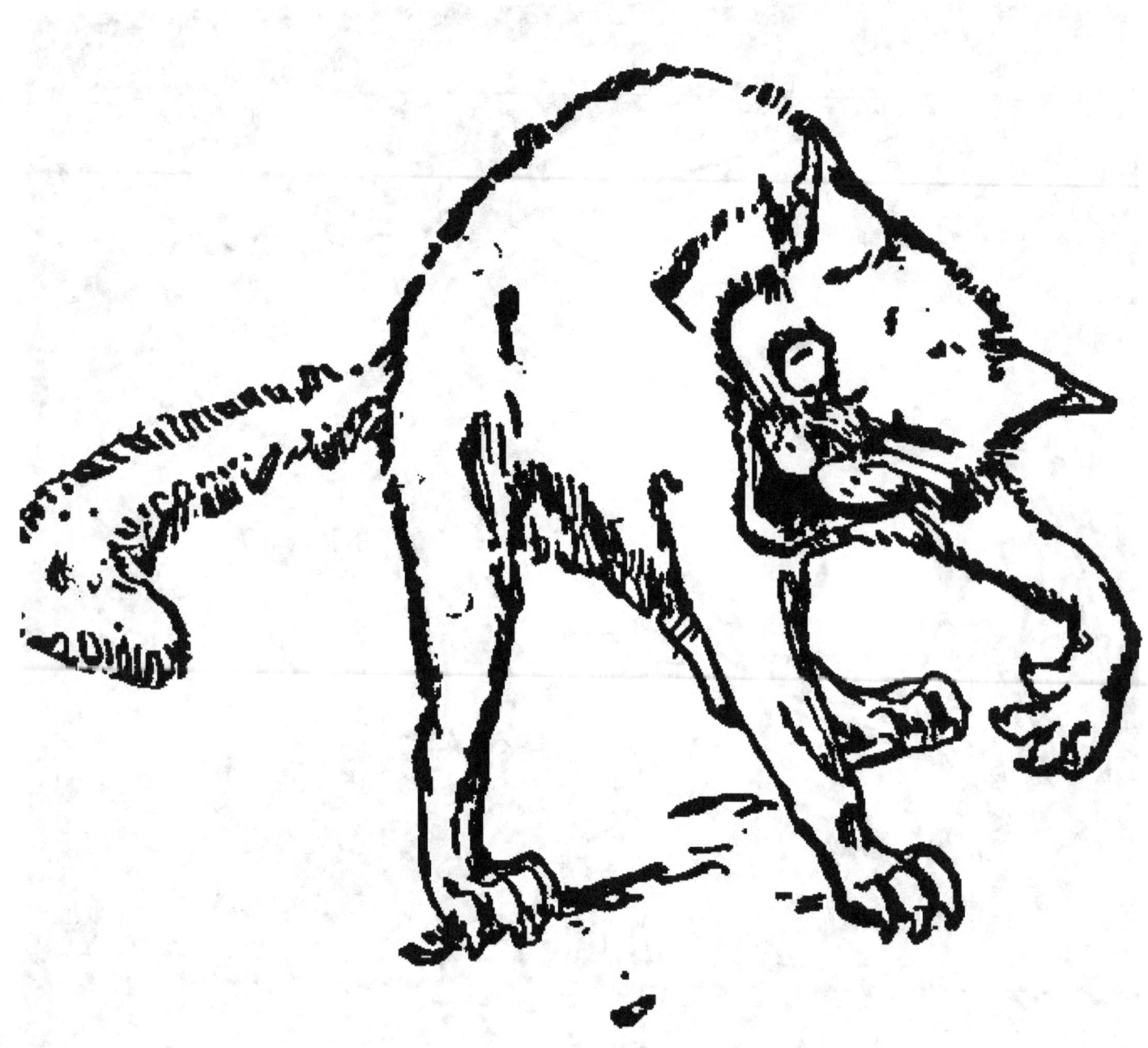

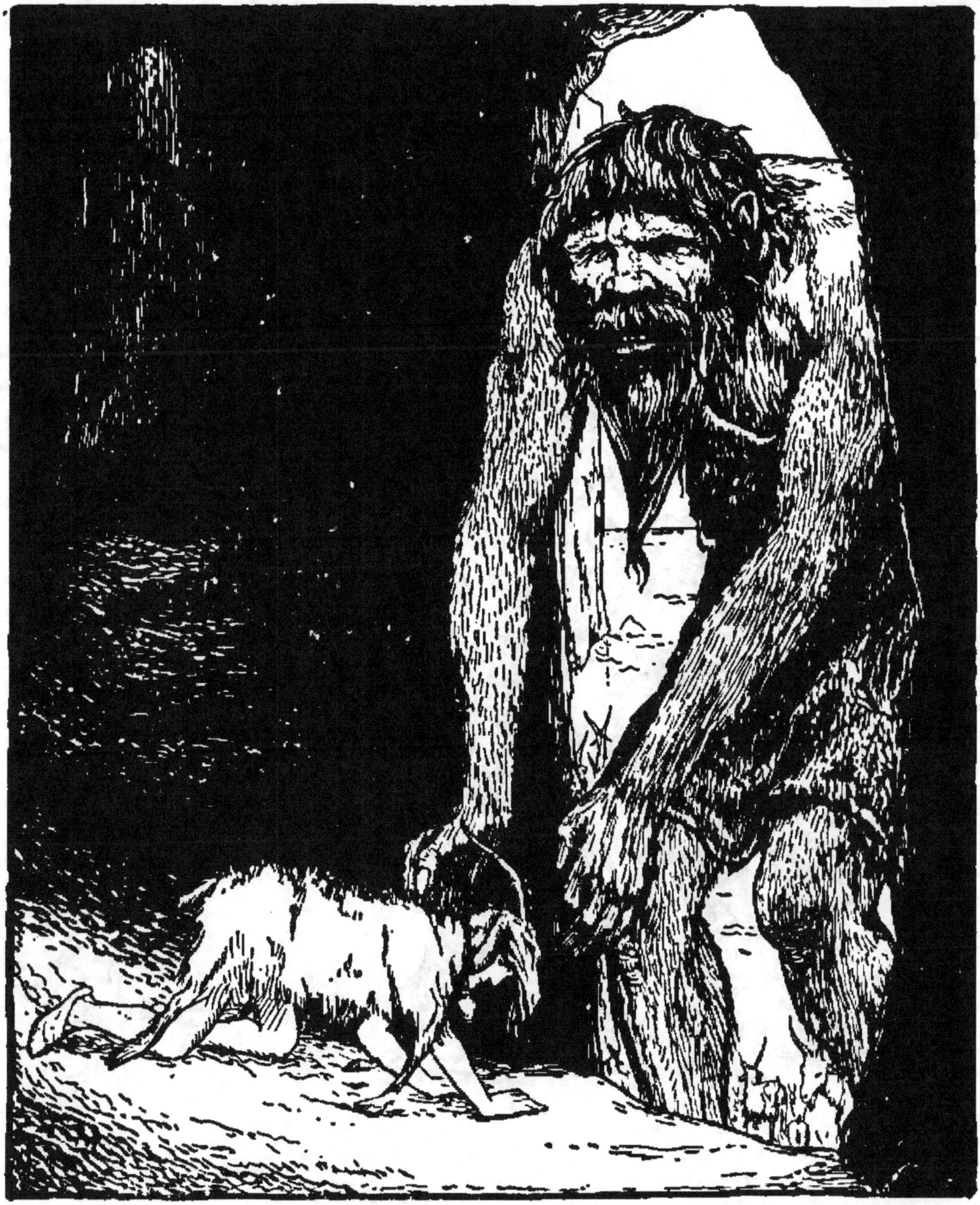

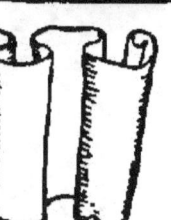

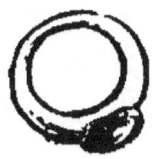  THERE THOU ART THOU PRETTY BUCK · THOU SEEST ME BUT I SEE THEE NOT

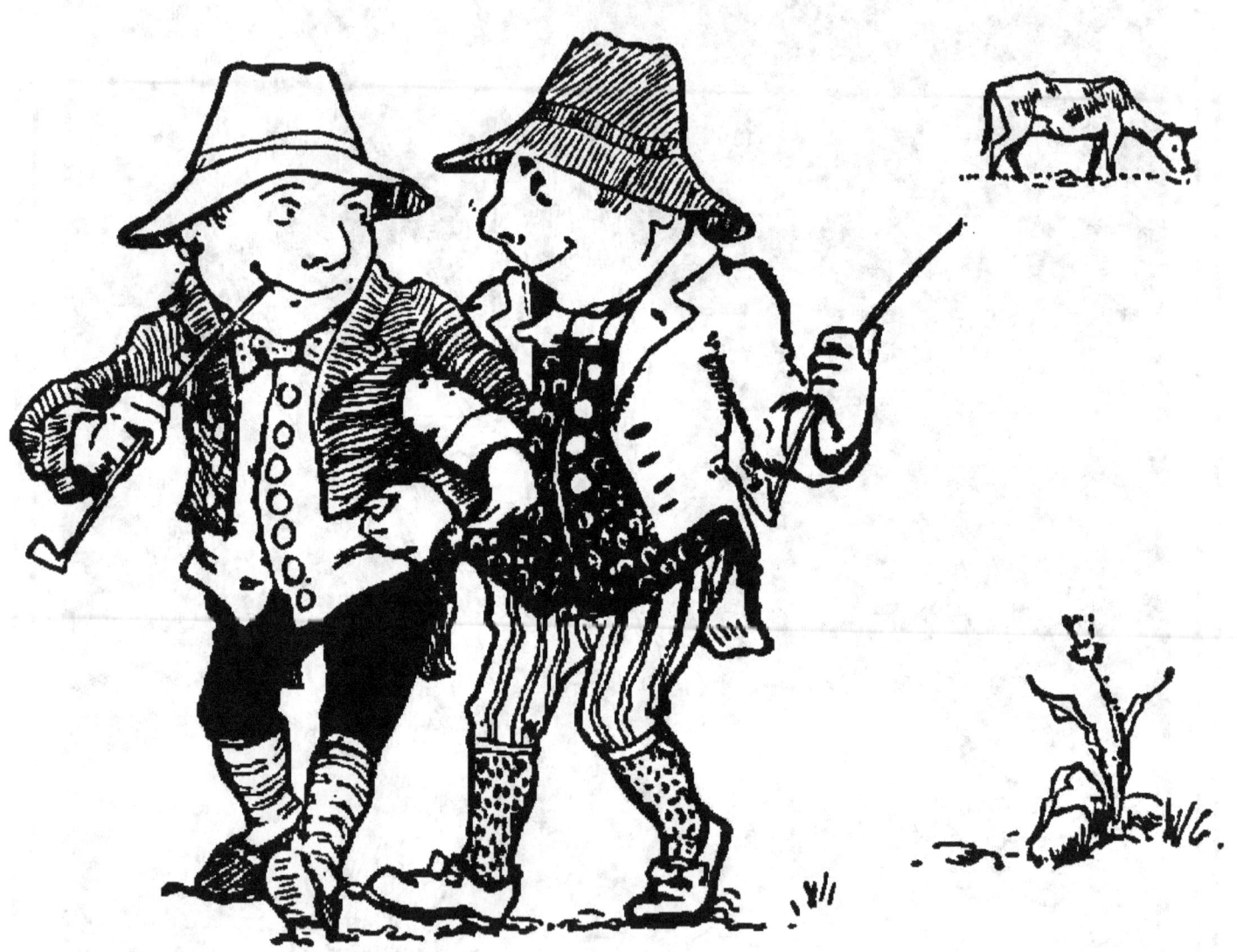

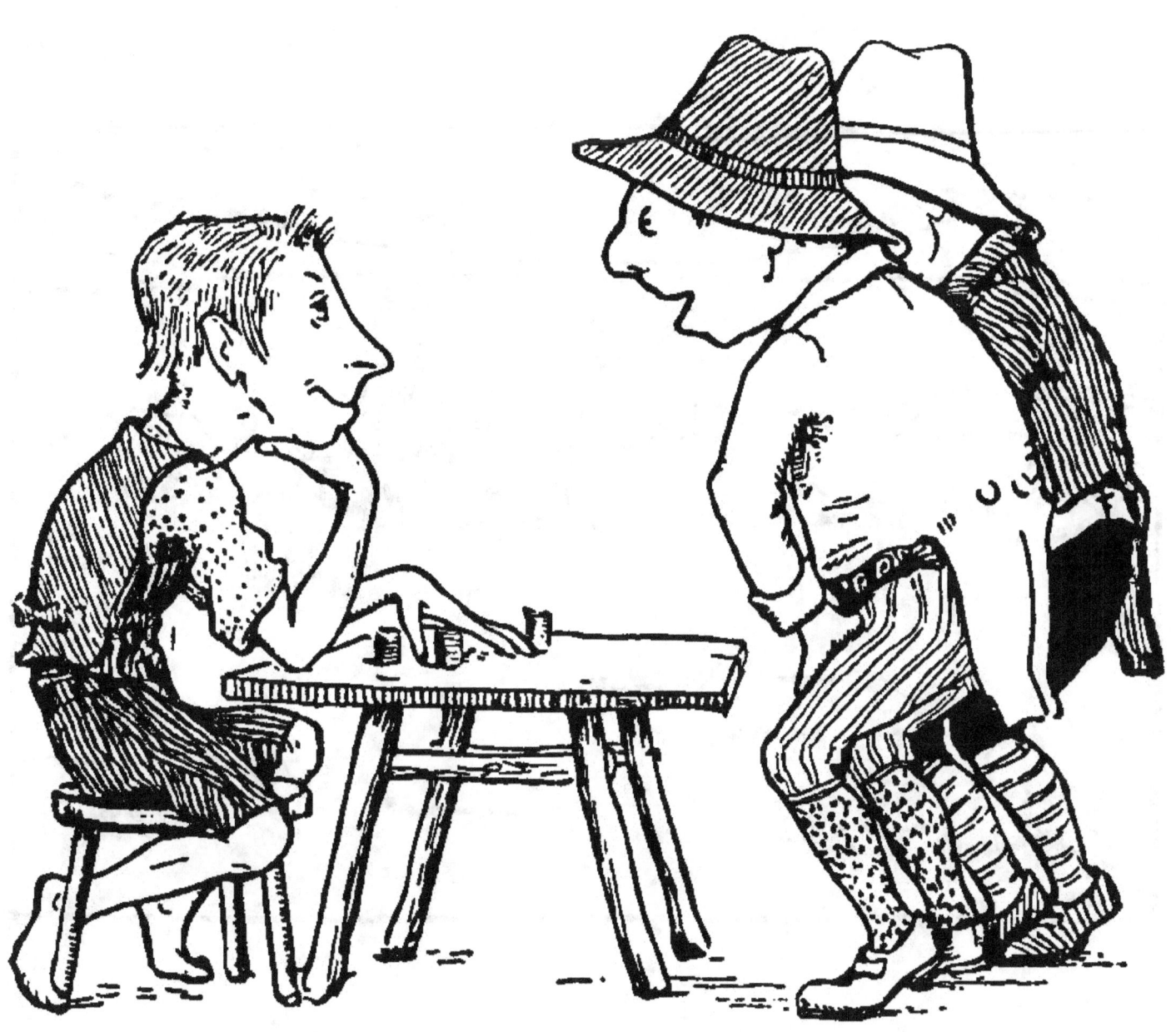

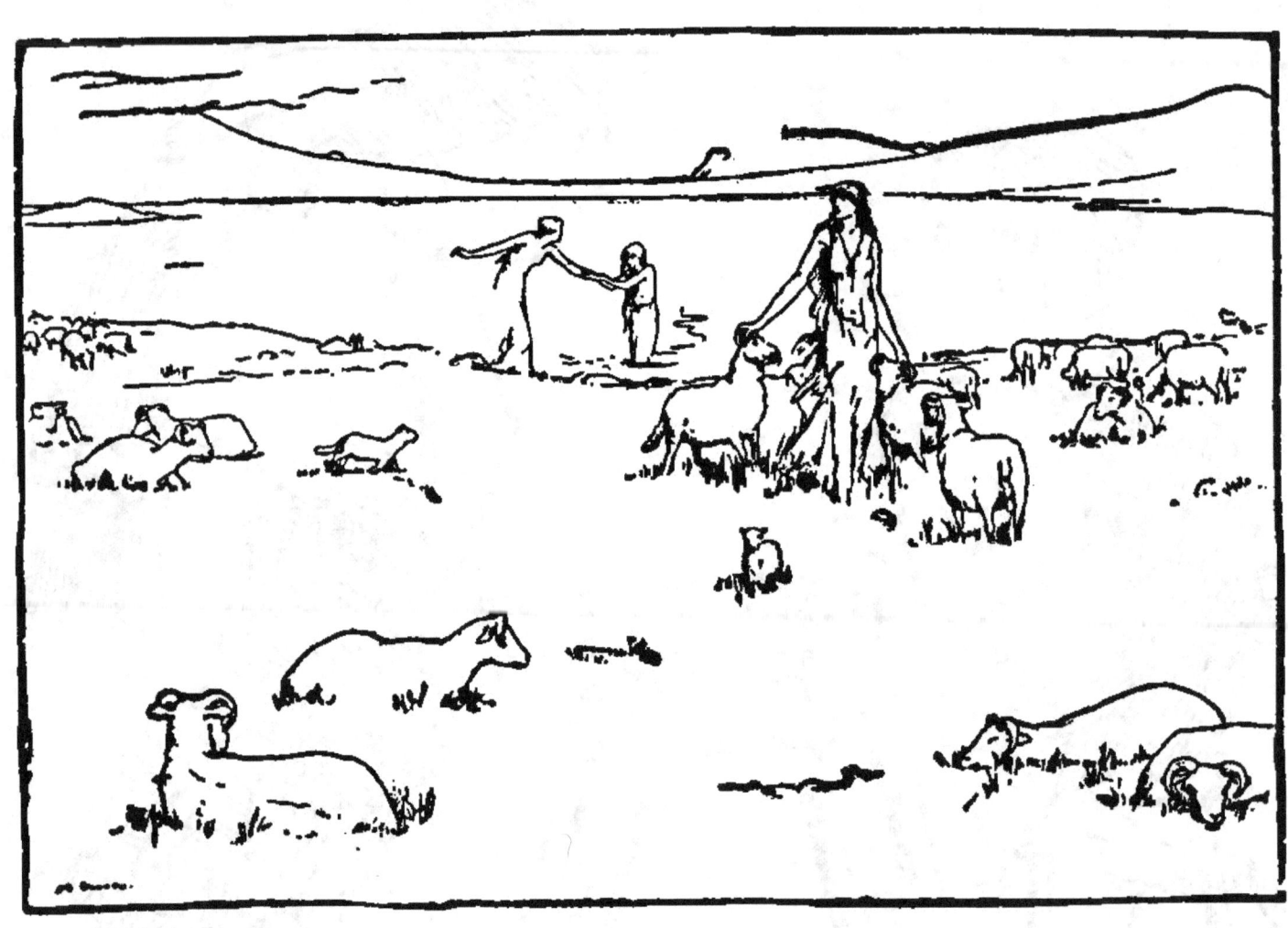

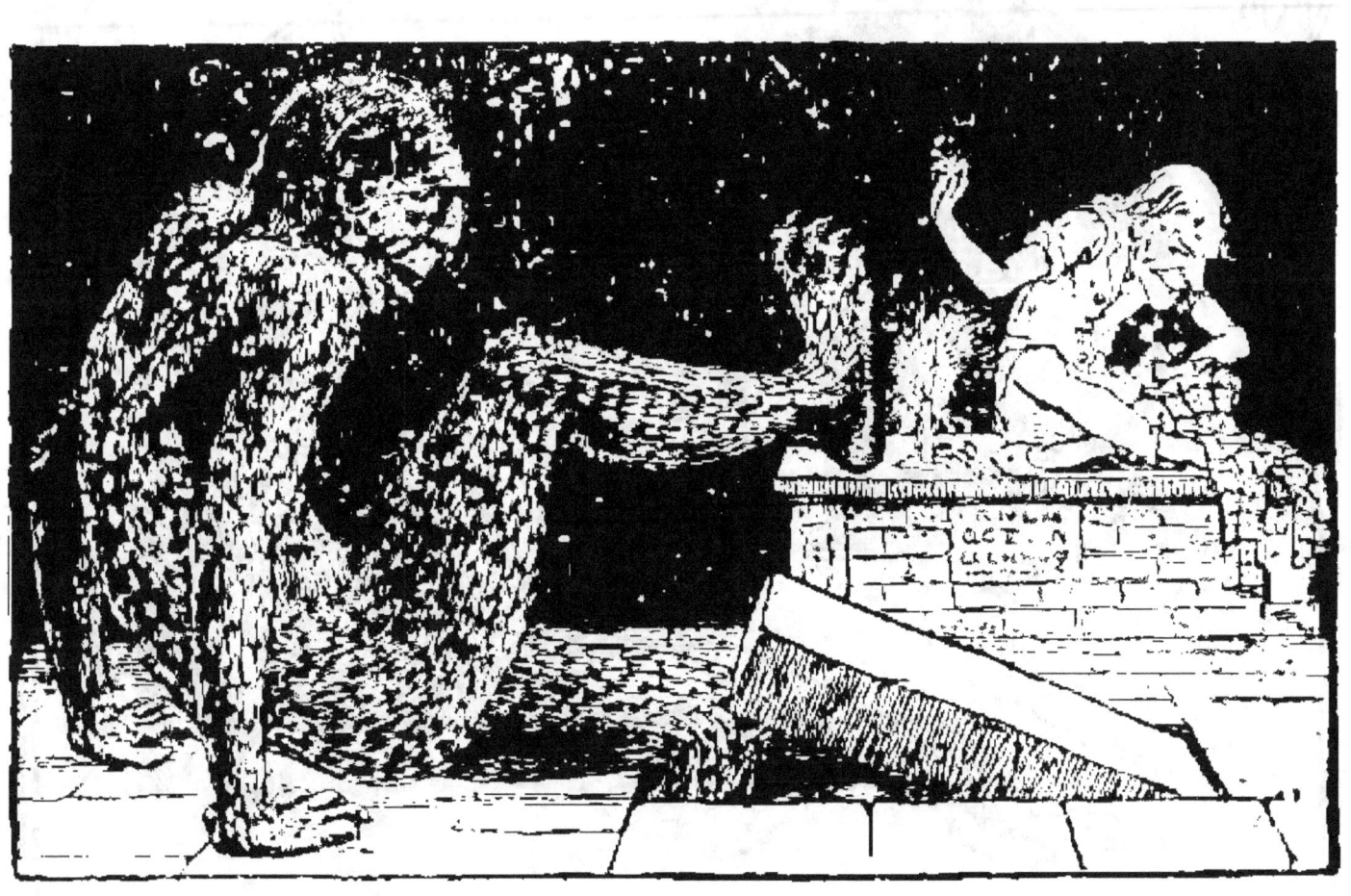

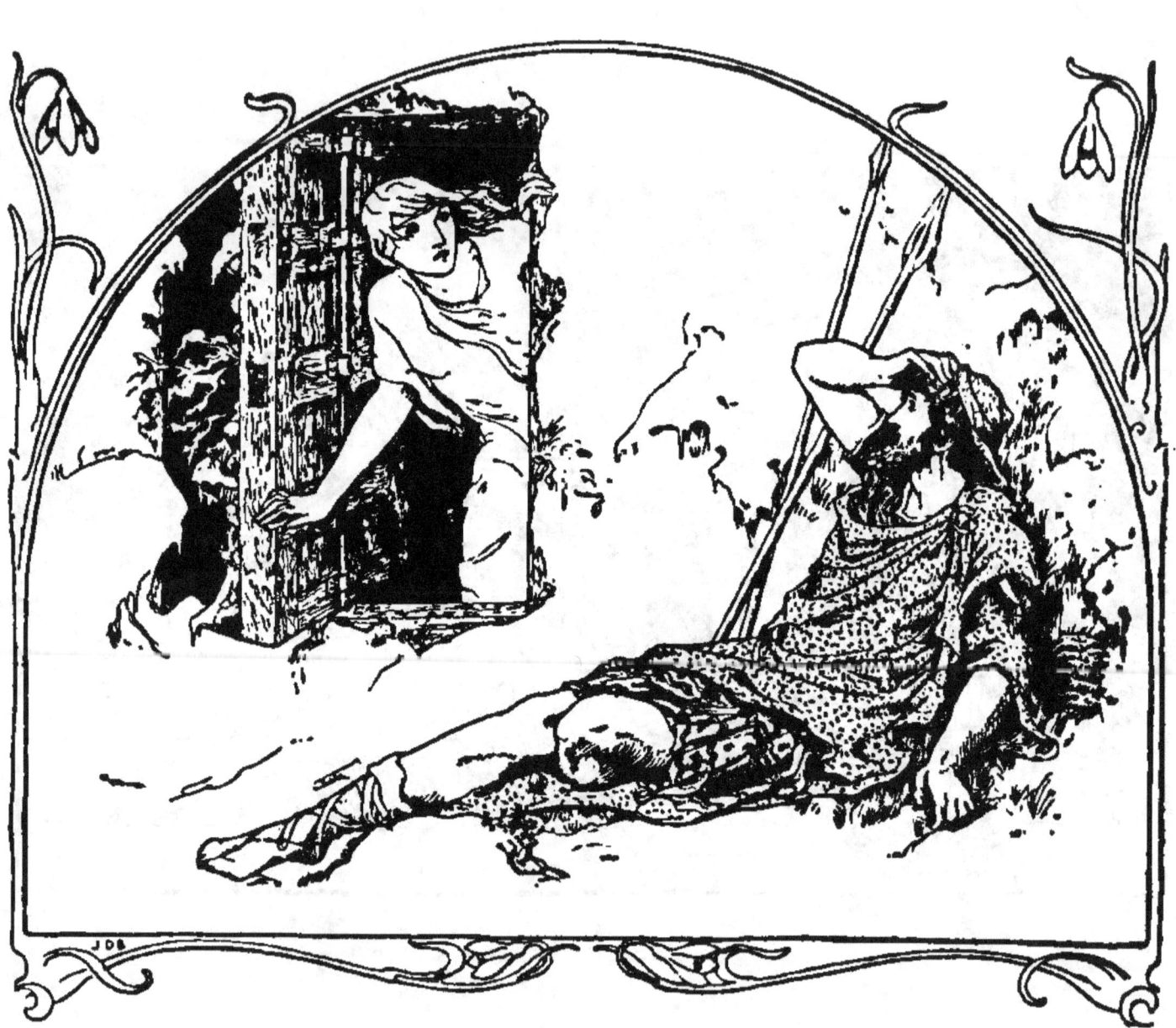

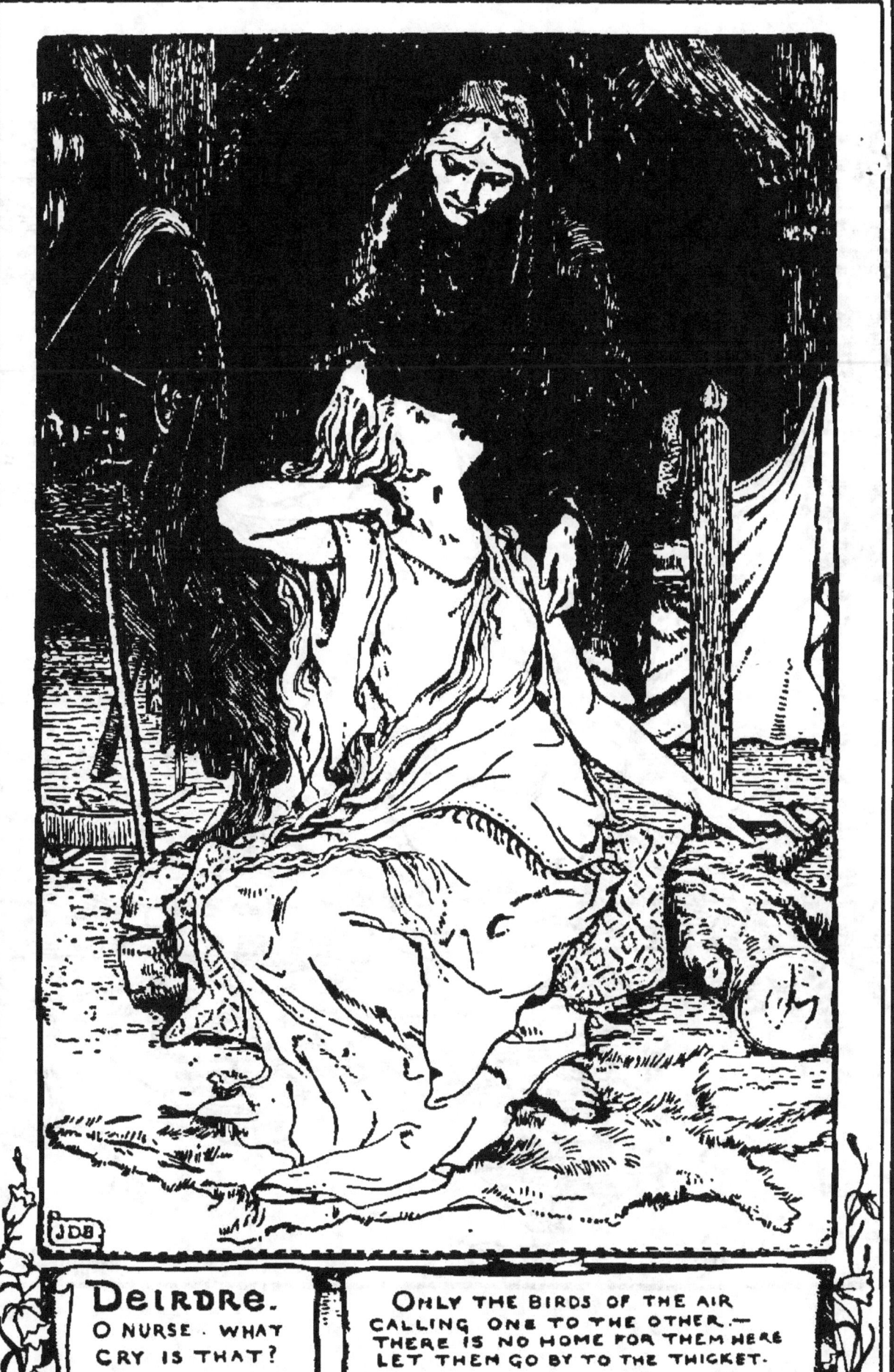

DeirDre.
O NURSE. WHAT
CRY IS THAT?

ONLY THE BIRDS OF THE AIR
CALLING ONE TO THE OTHER.—
THERE IS NO HOME FOR THEM HERE
LET THEM GO BY TO THE THICKET.

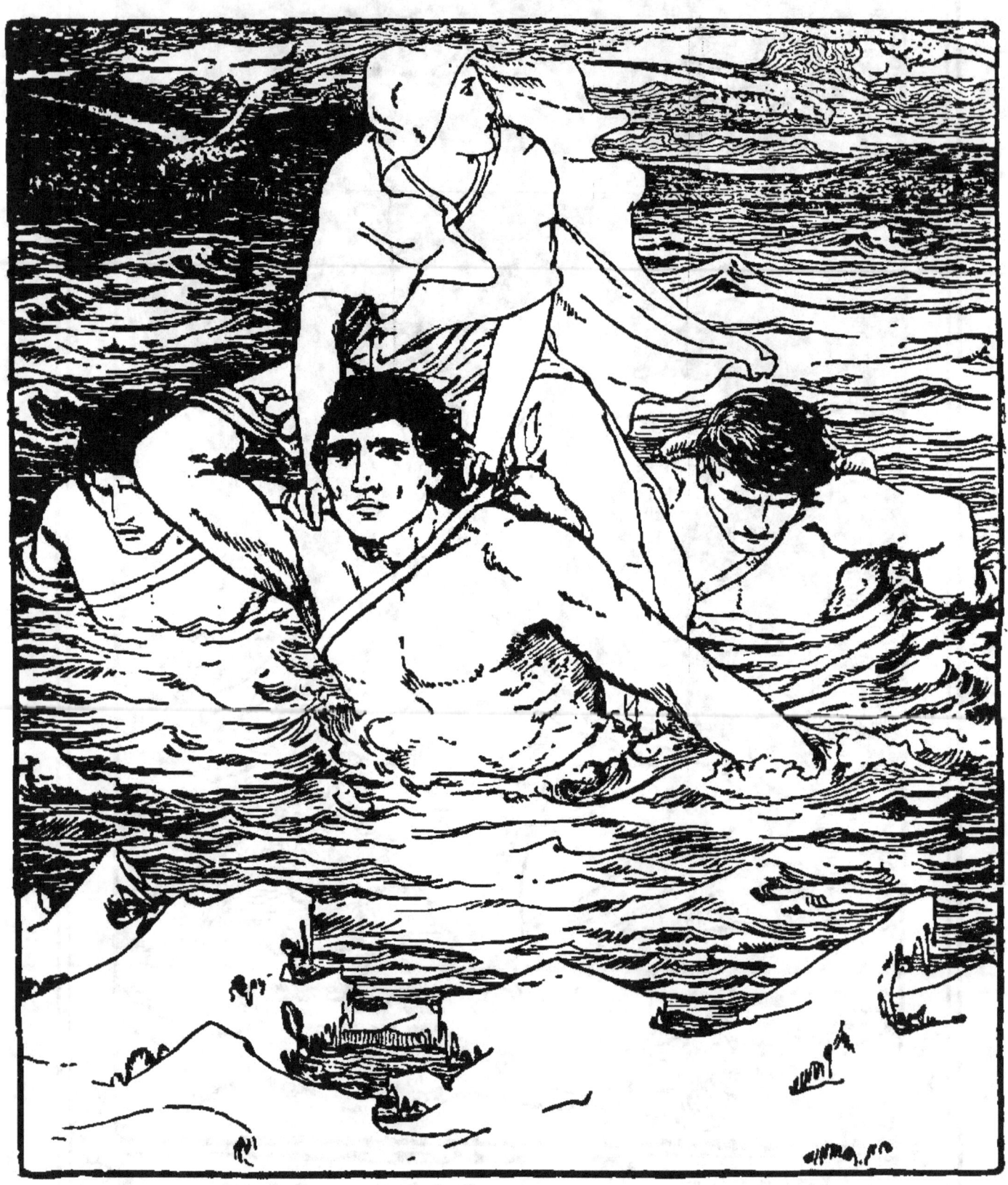

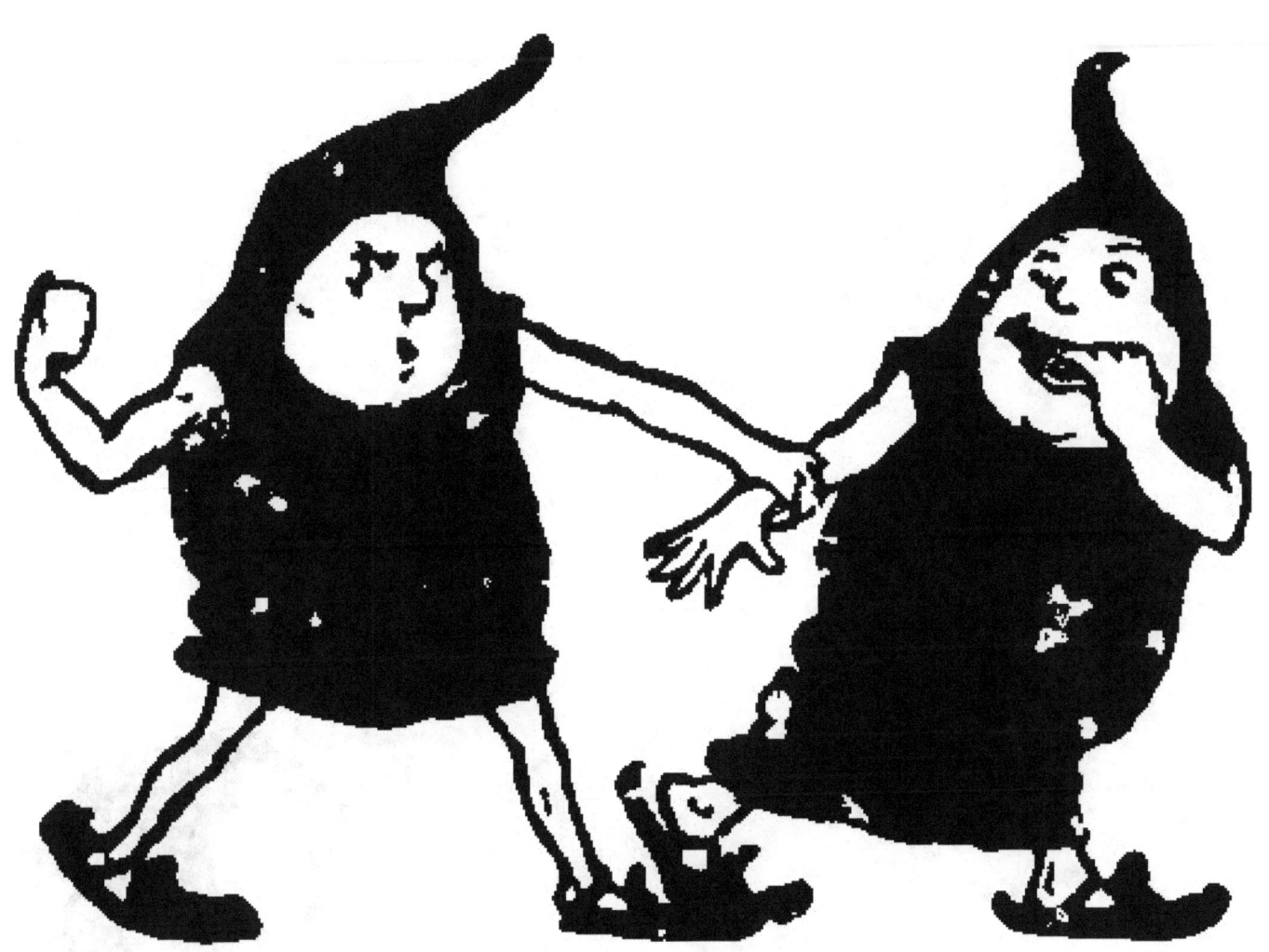

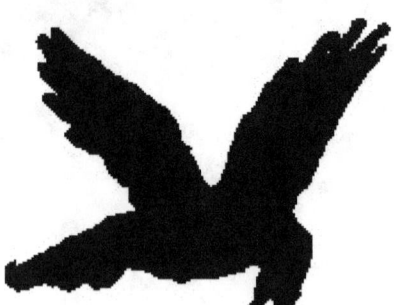

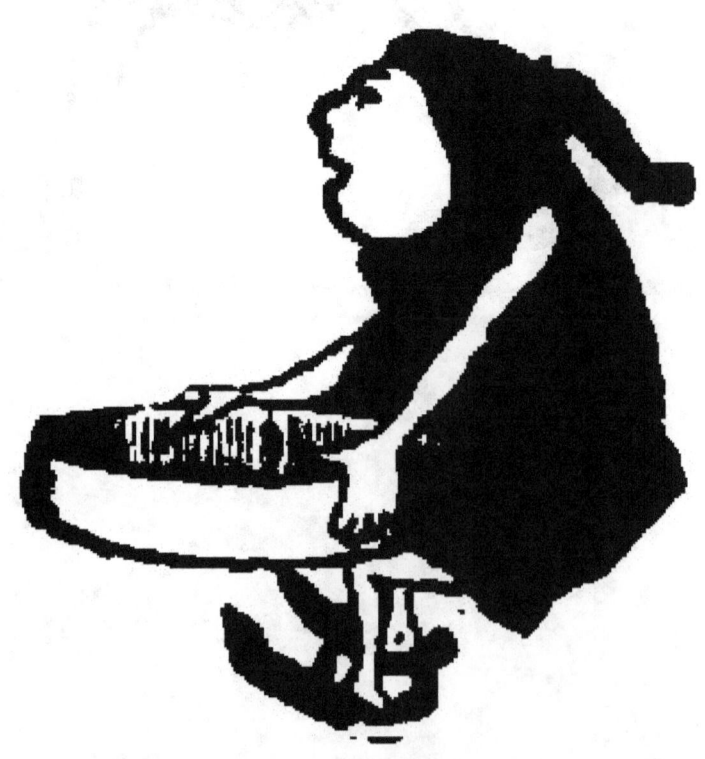

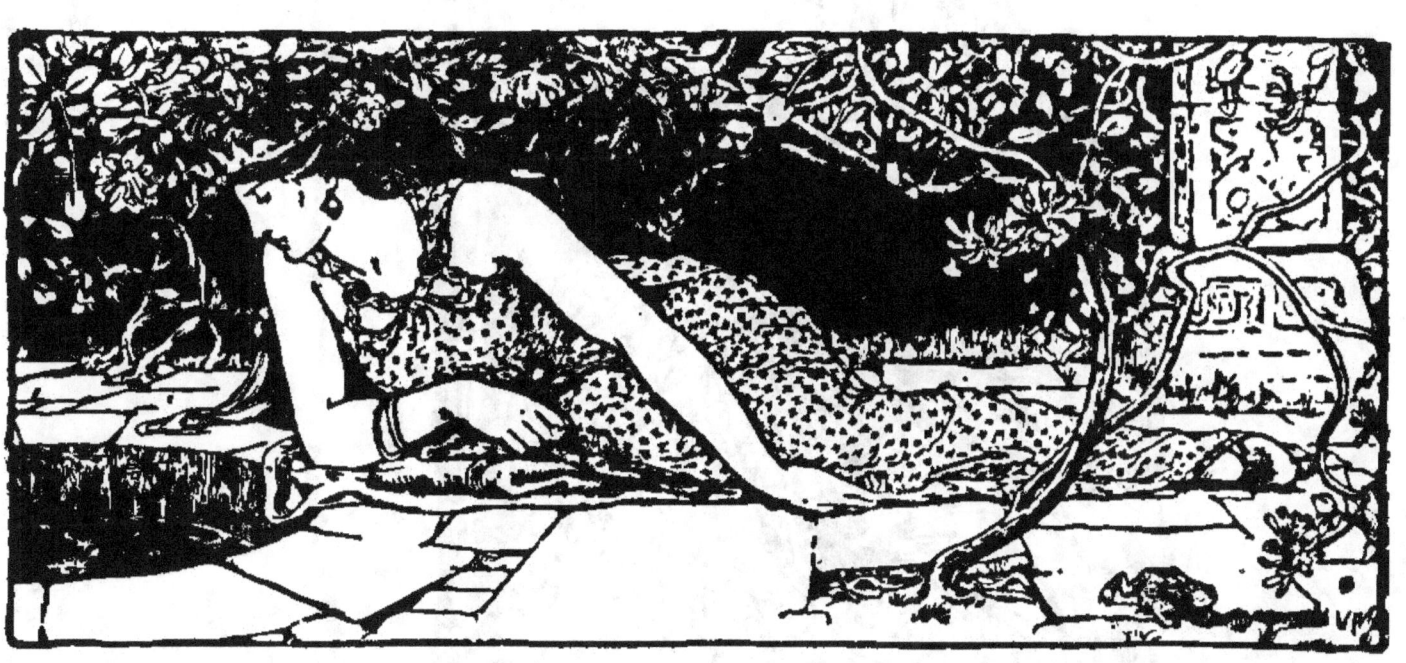

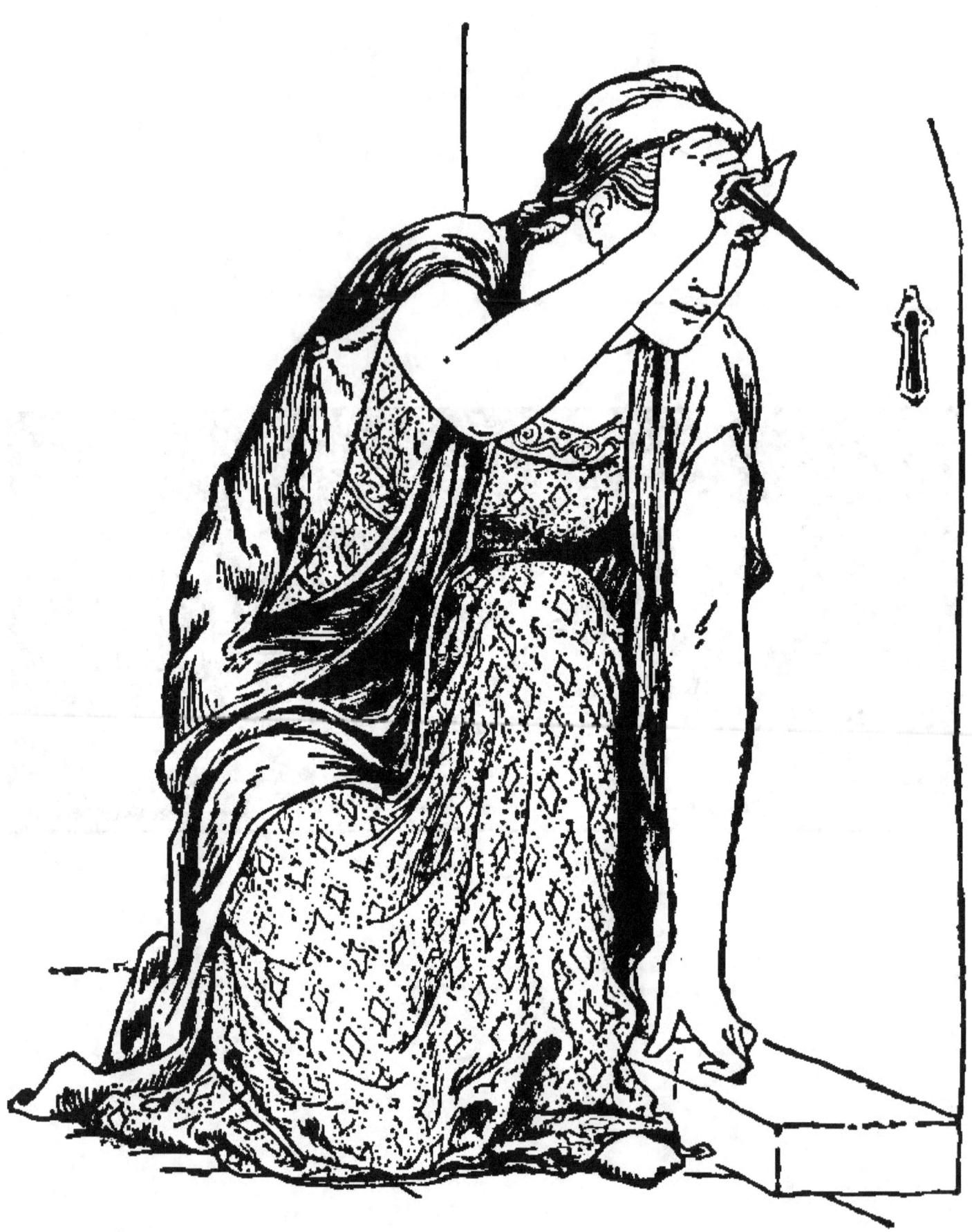

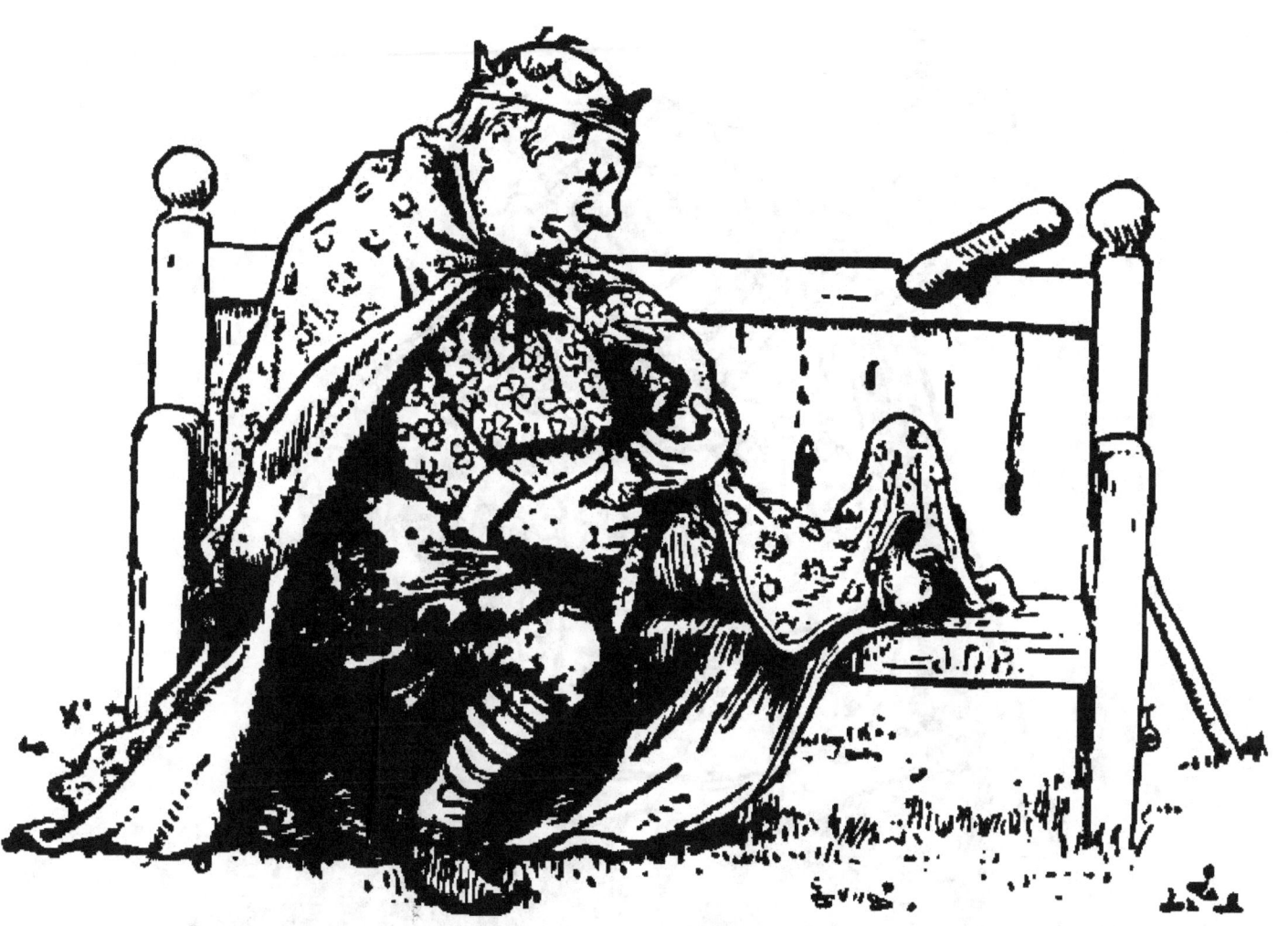

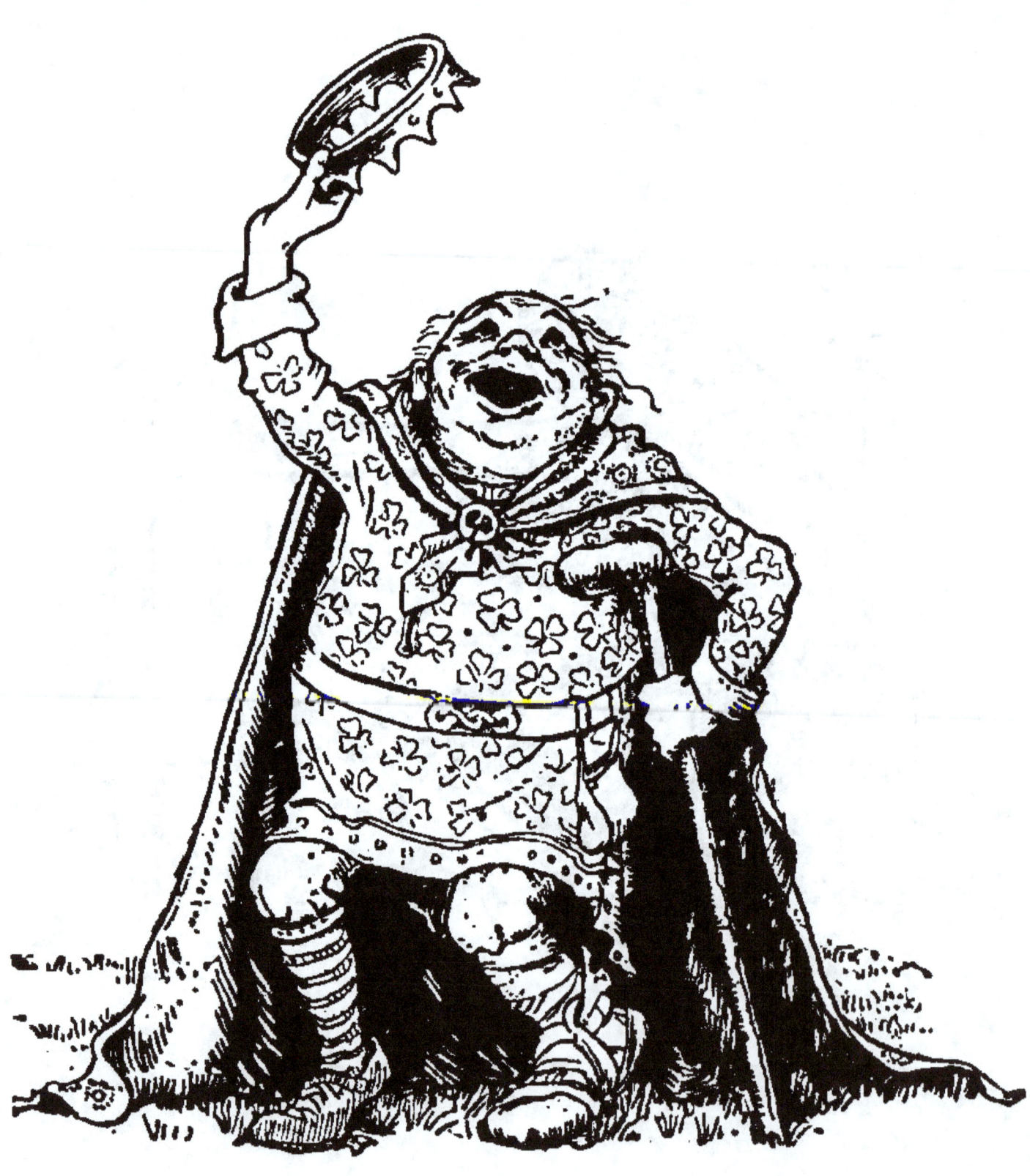

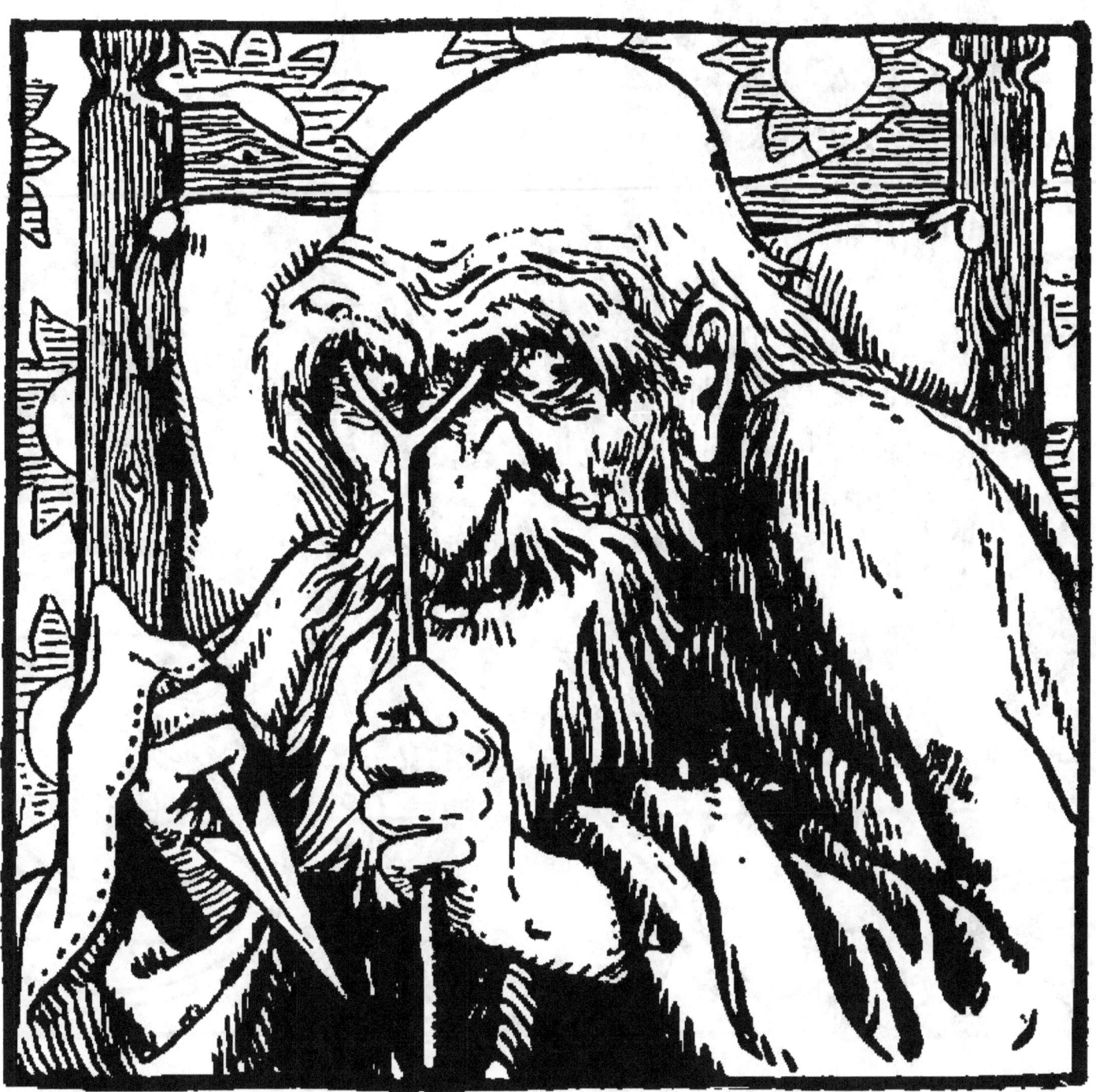

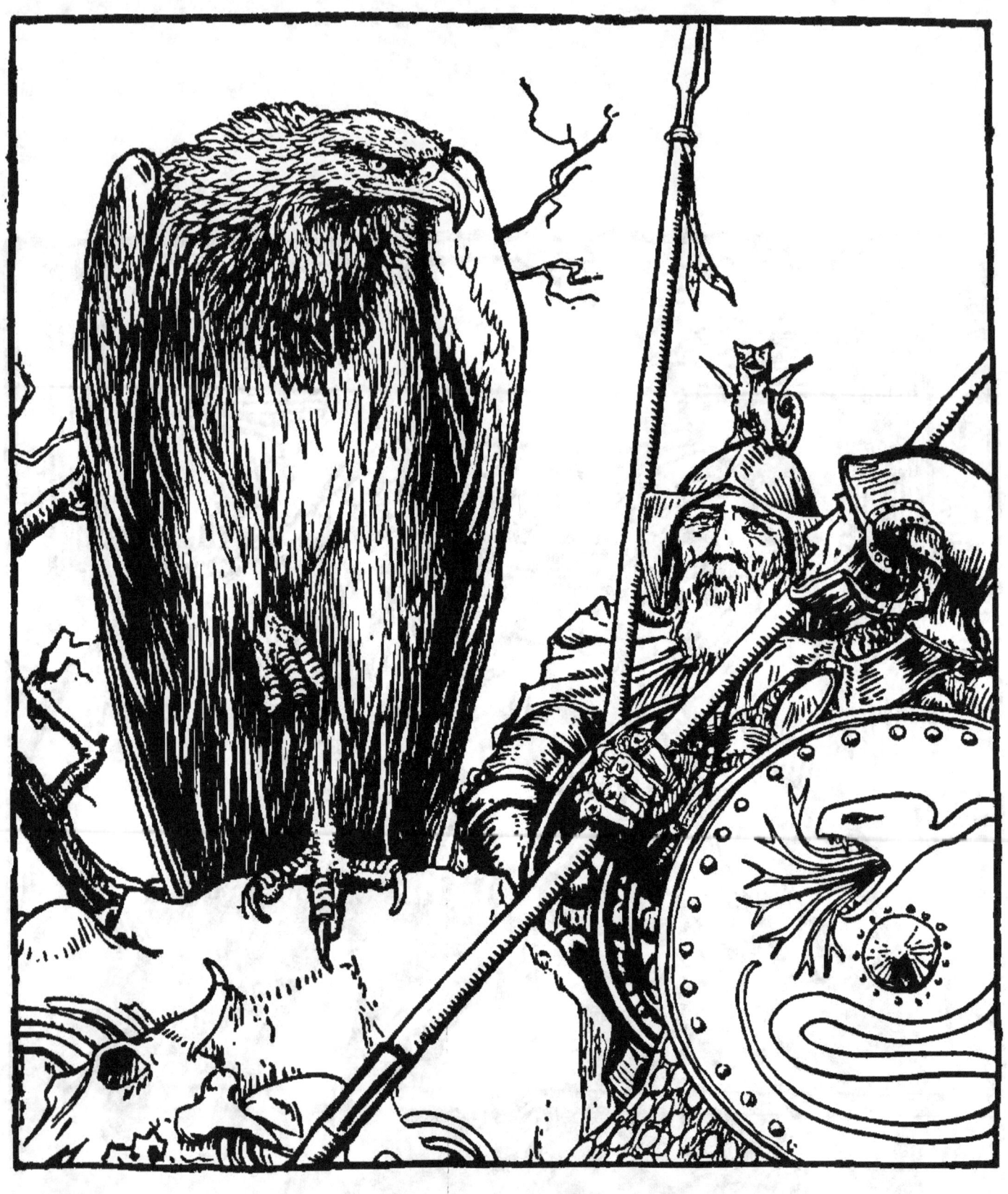

Gwrhyr and Eidoel talk with the Eagle of Gwern Abwy

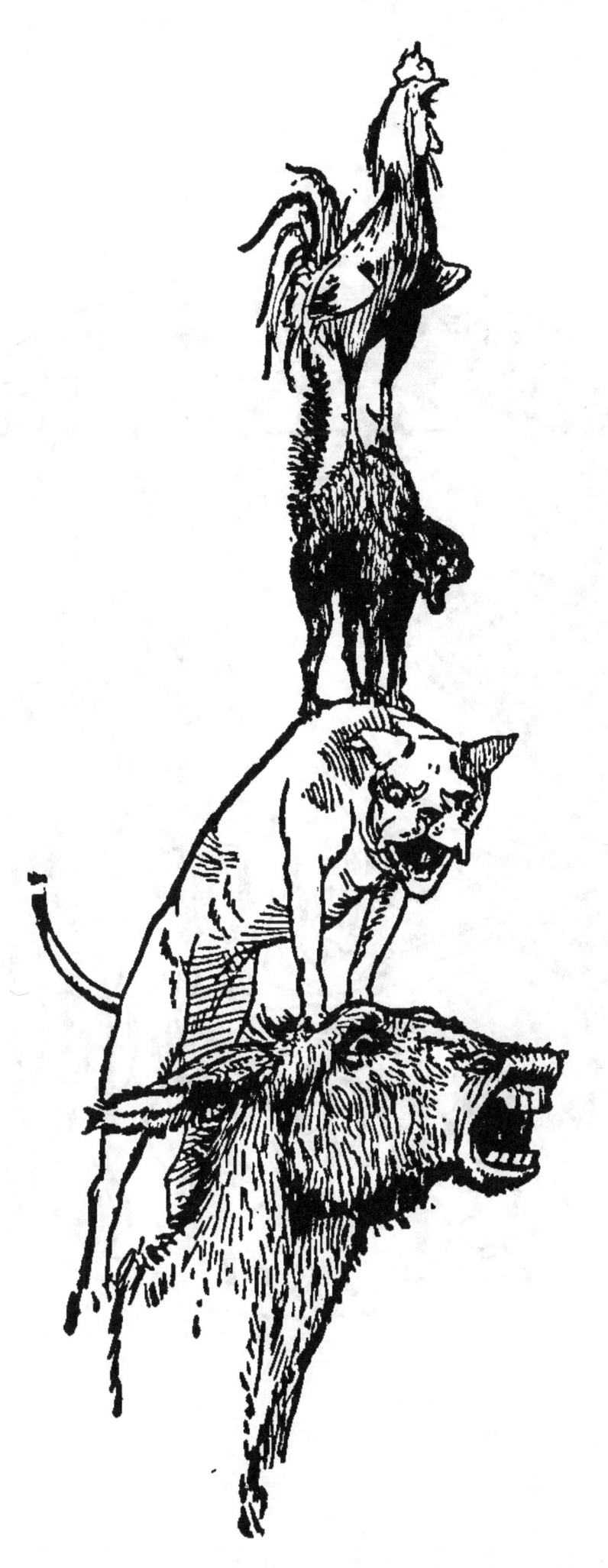

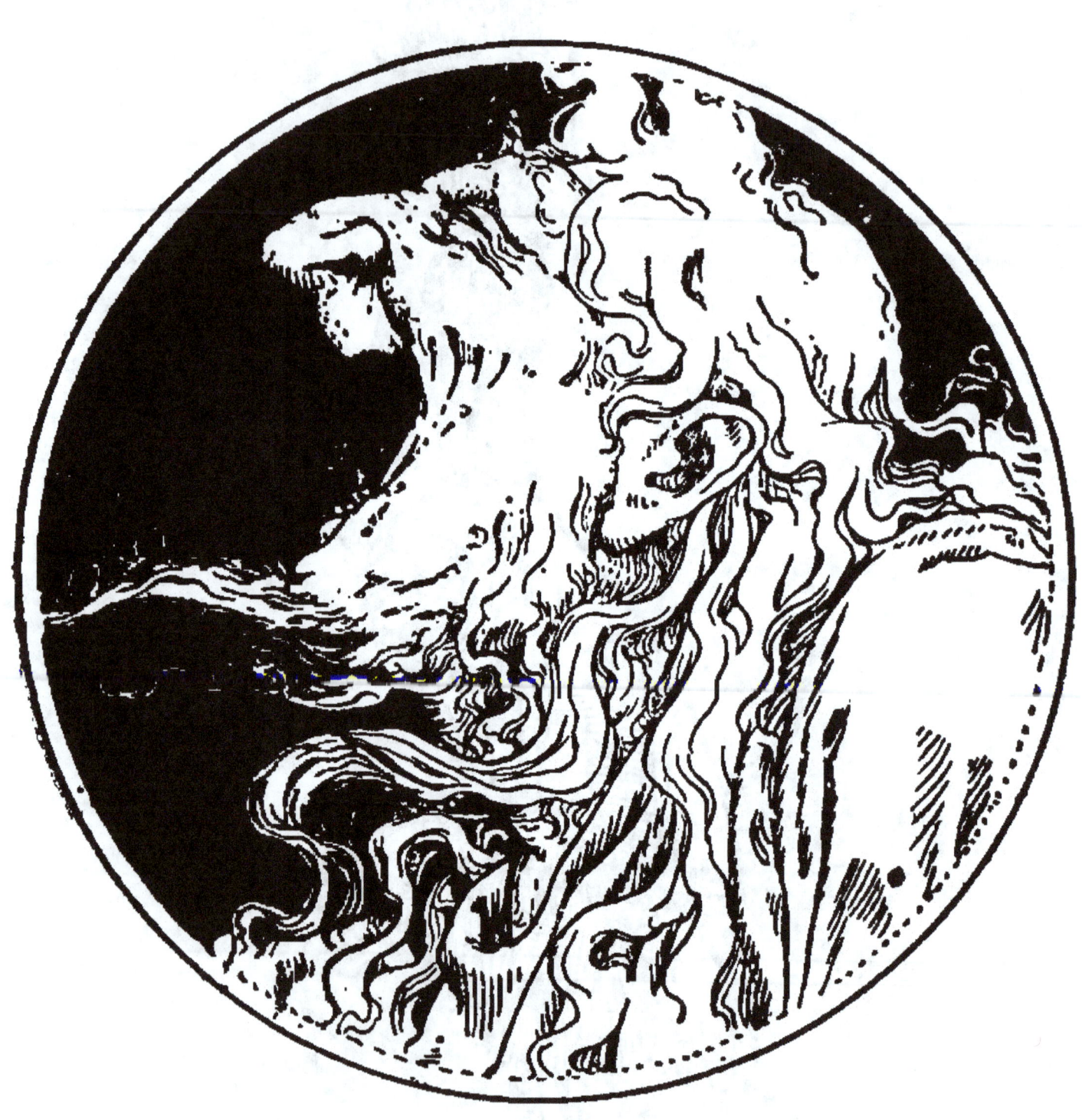

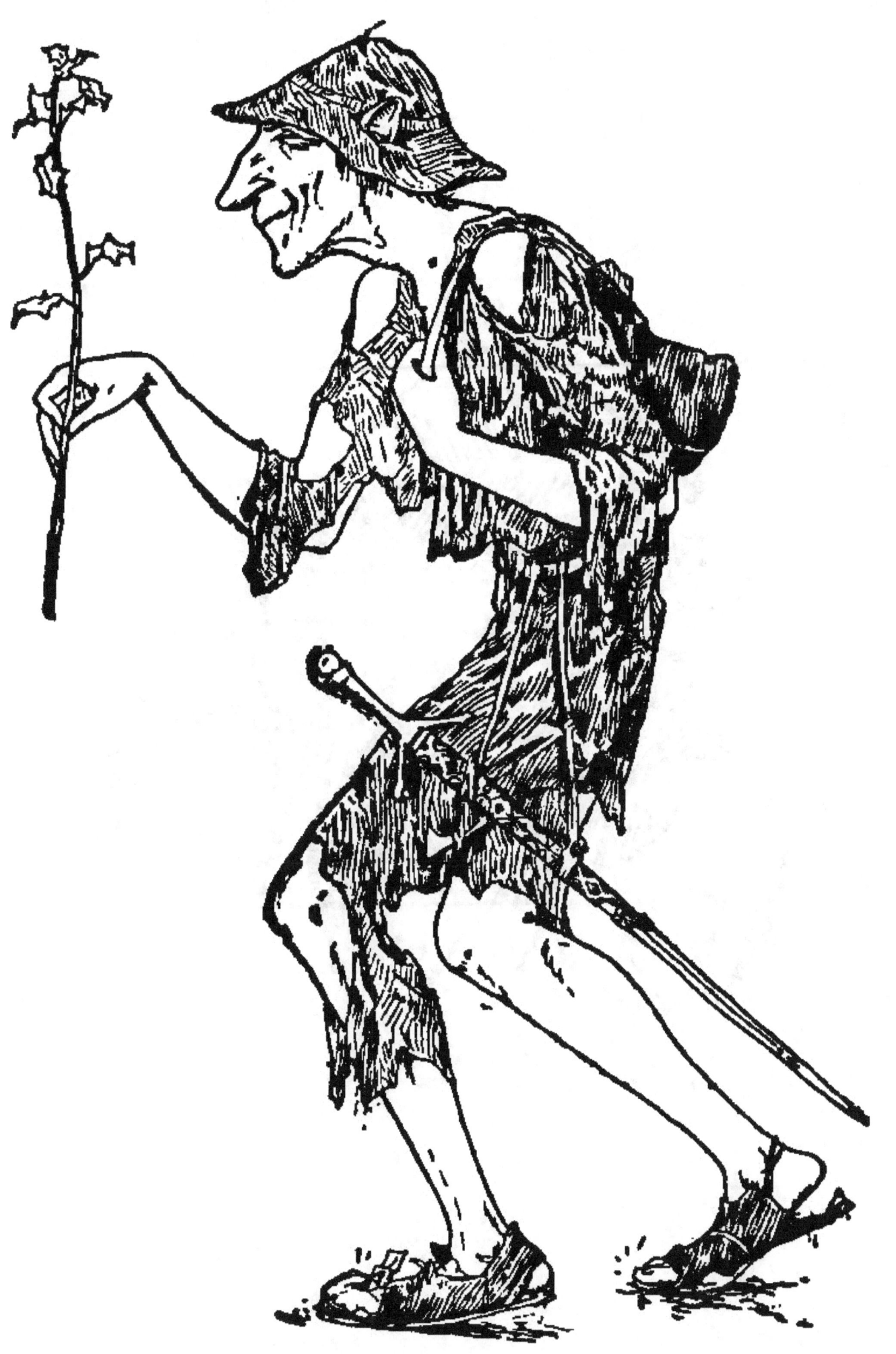

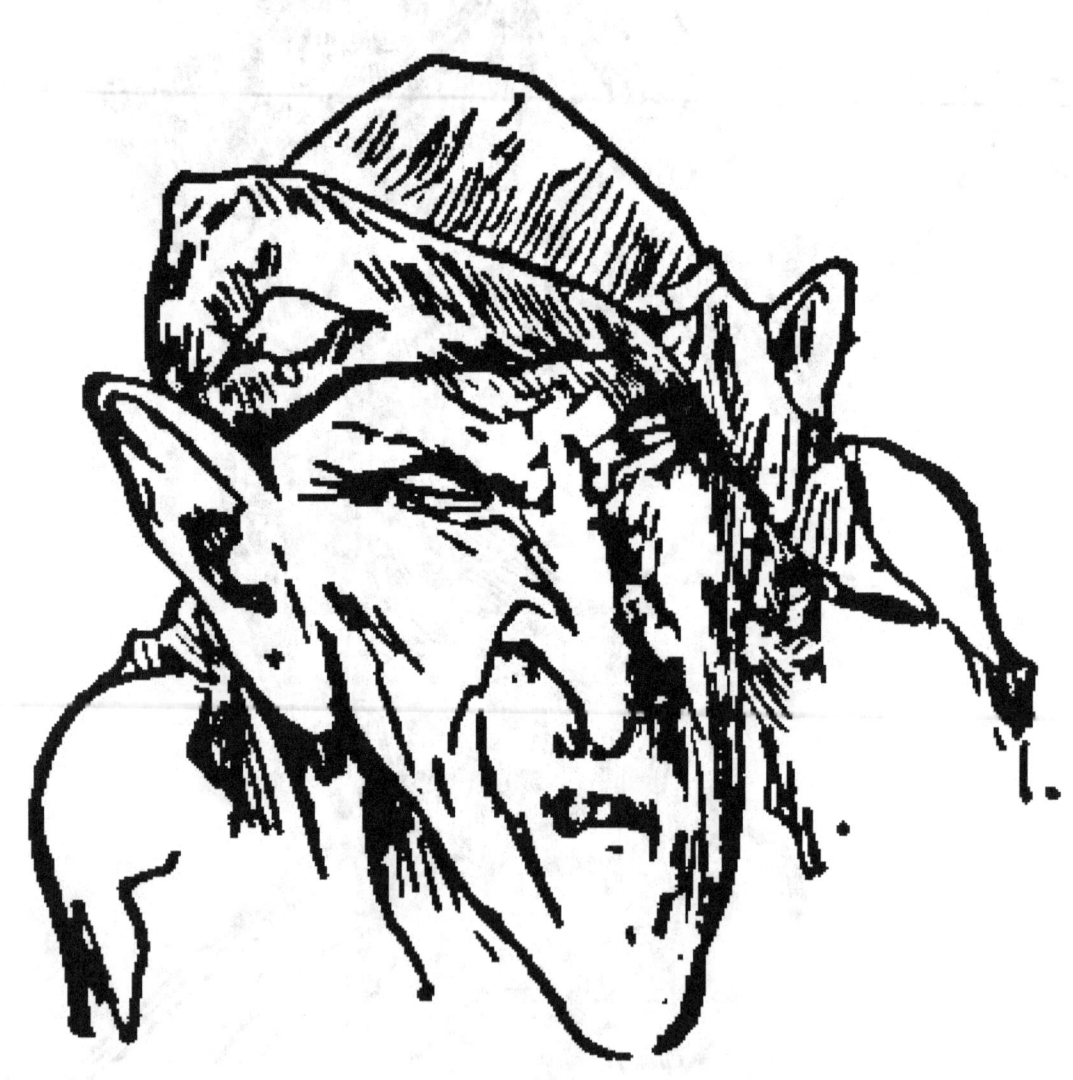

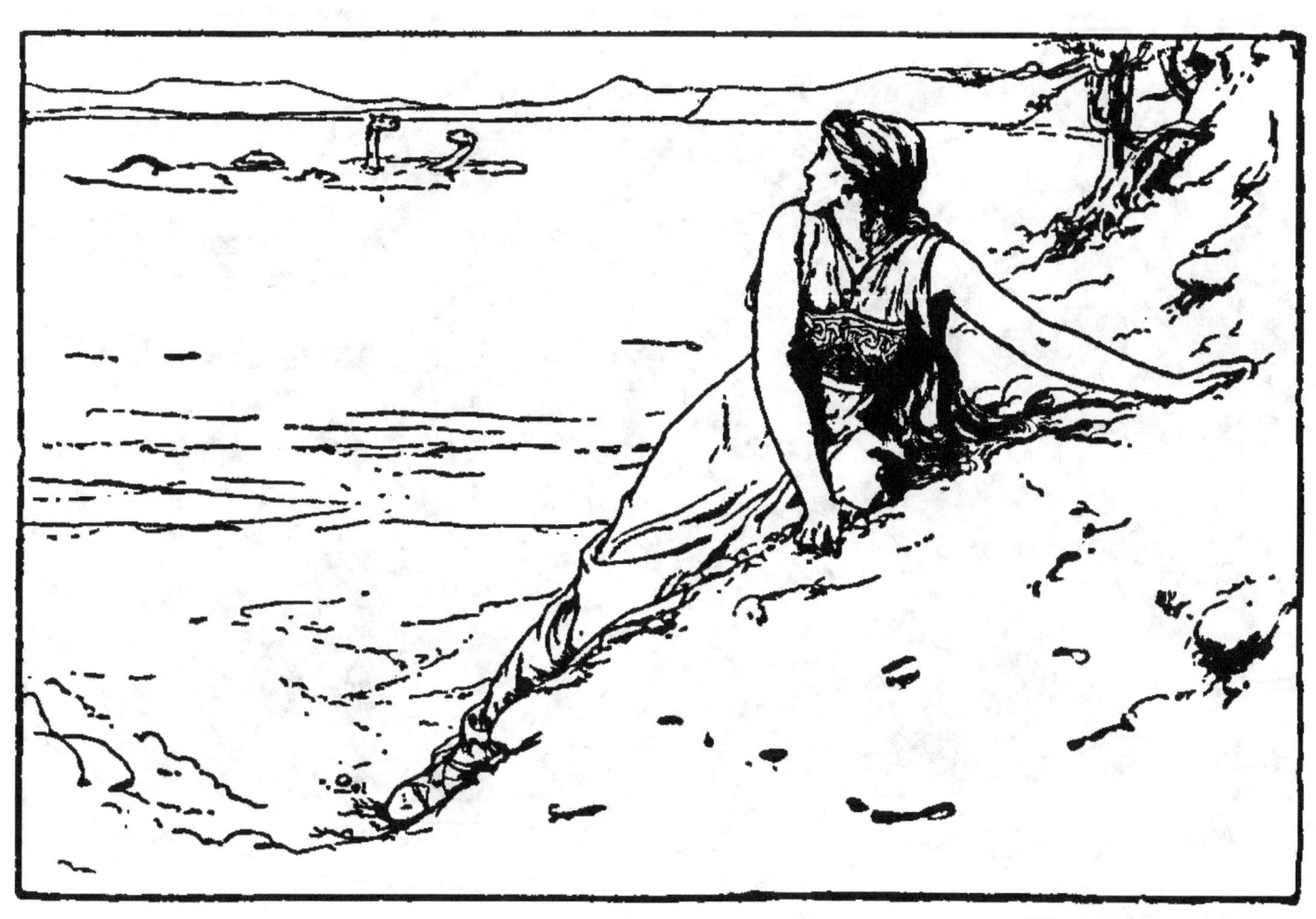

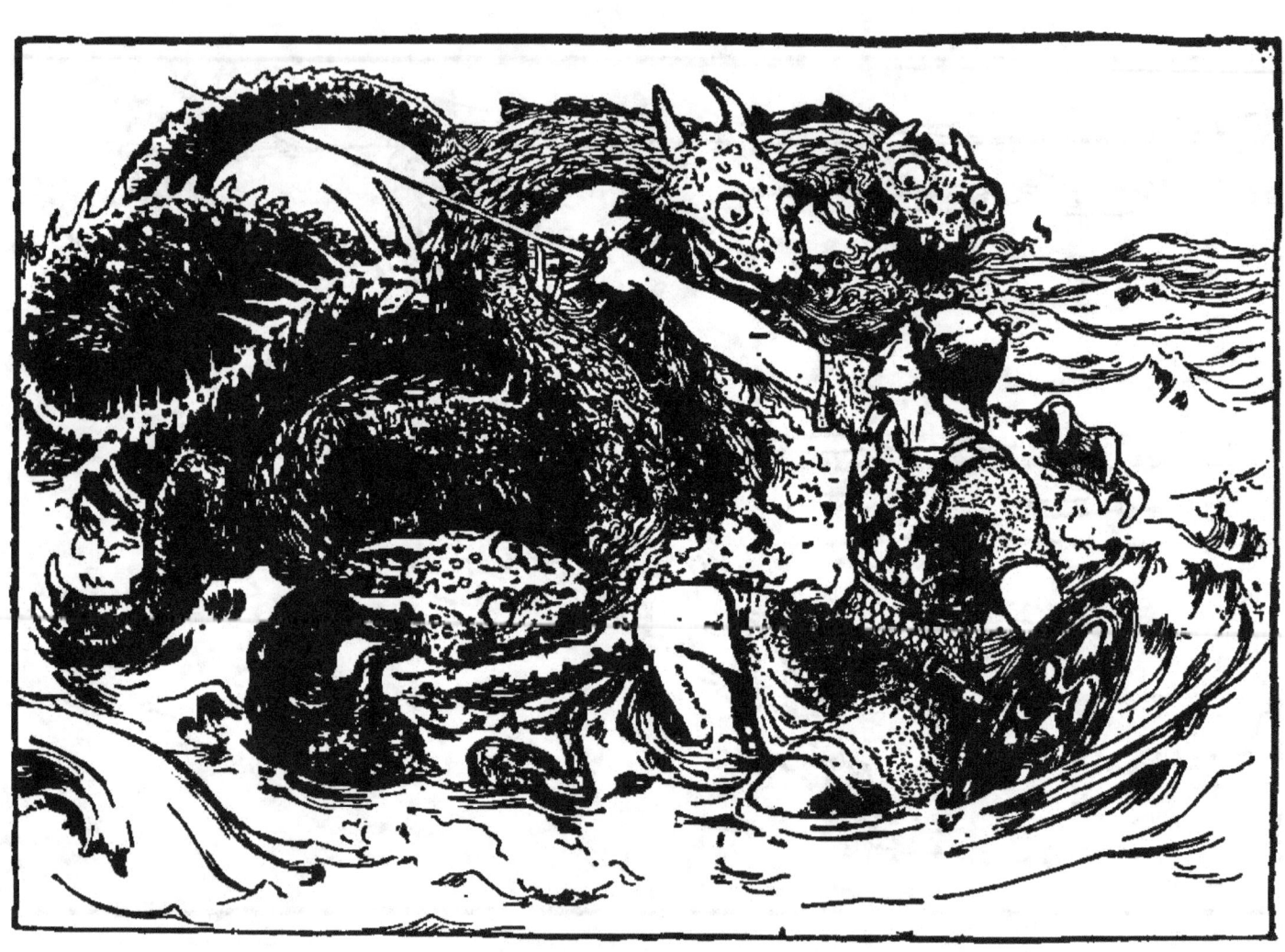

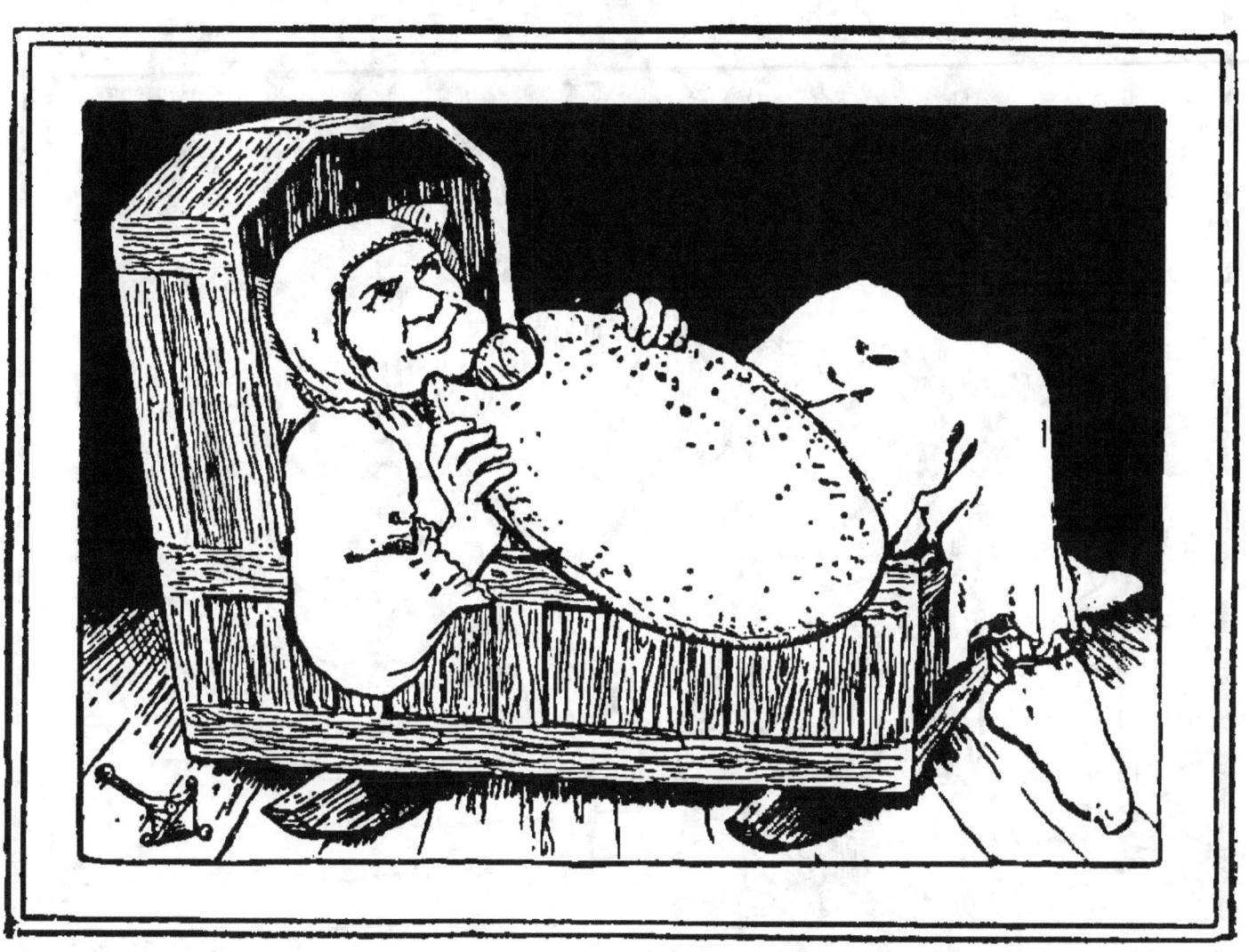

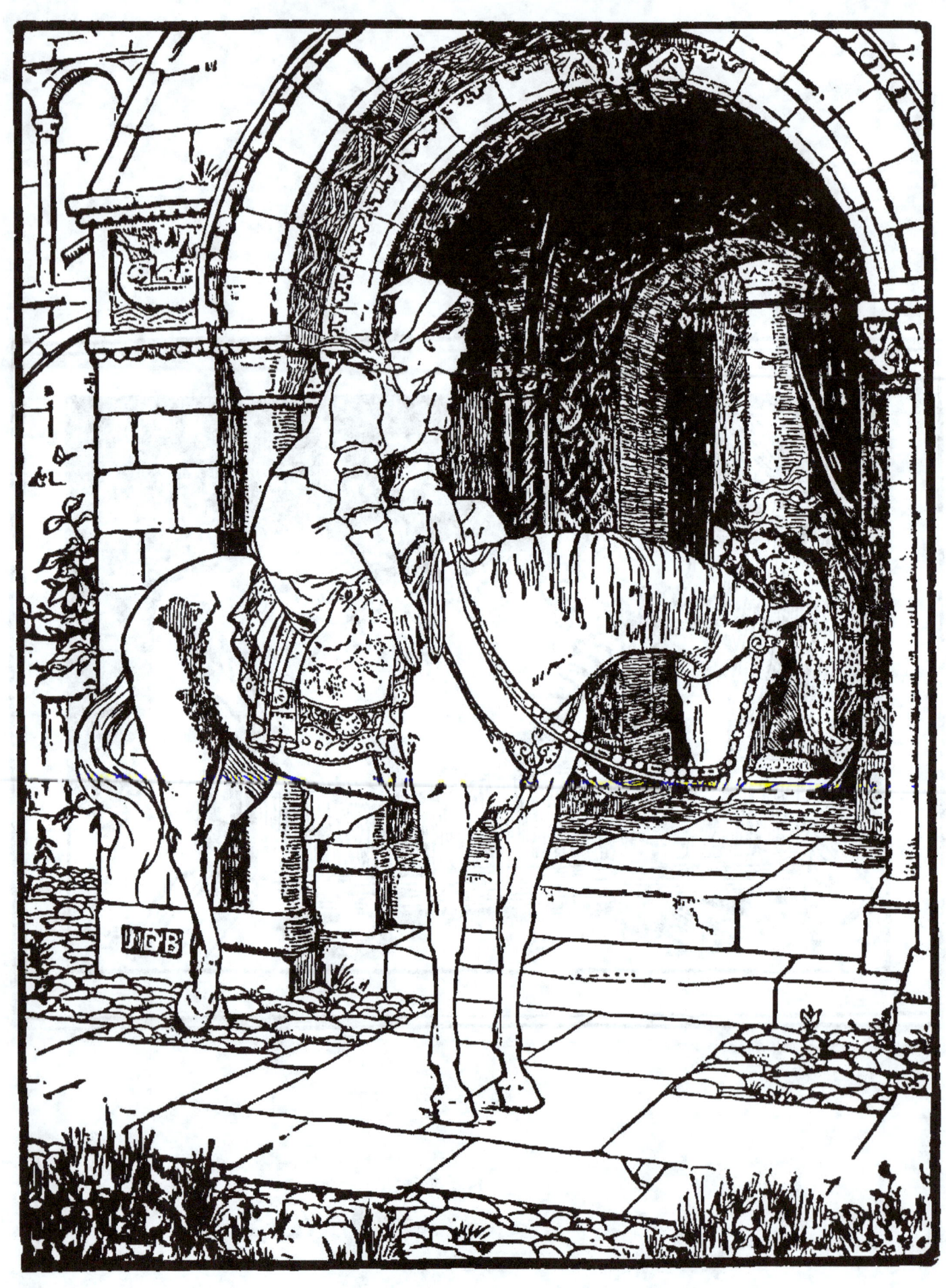

"*TREMBLING*" *AT THE CHURCH DOOR*

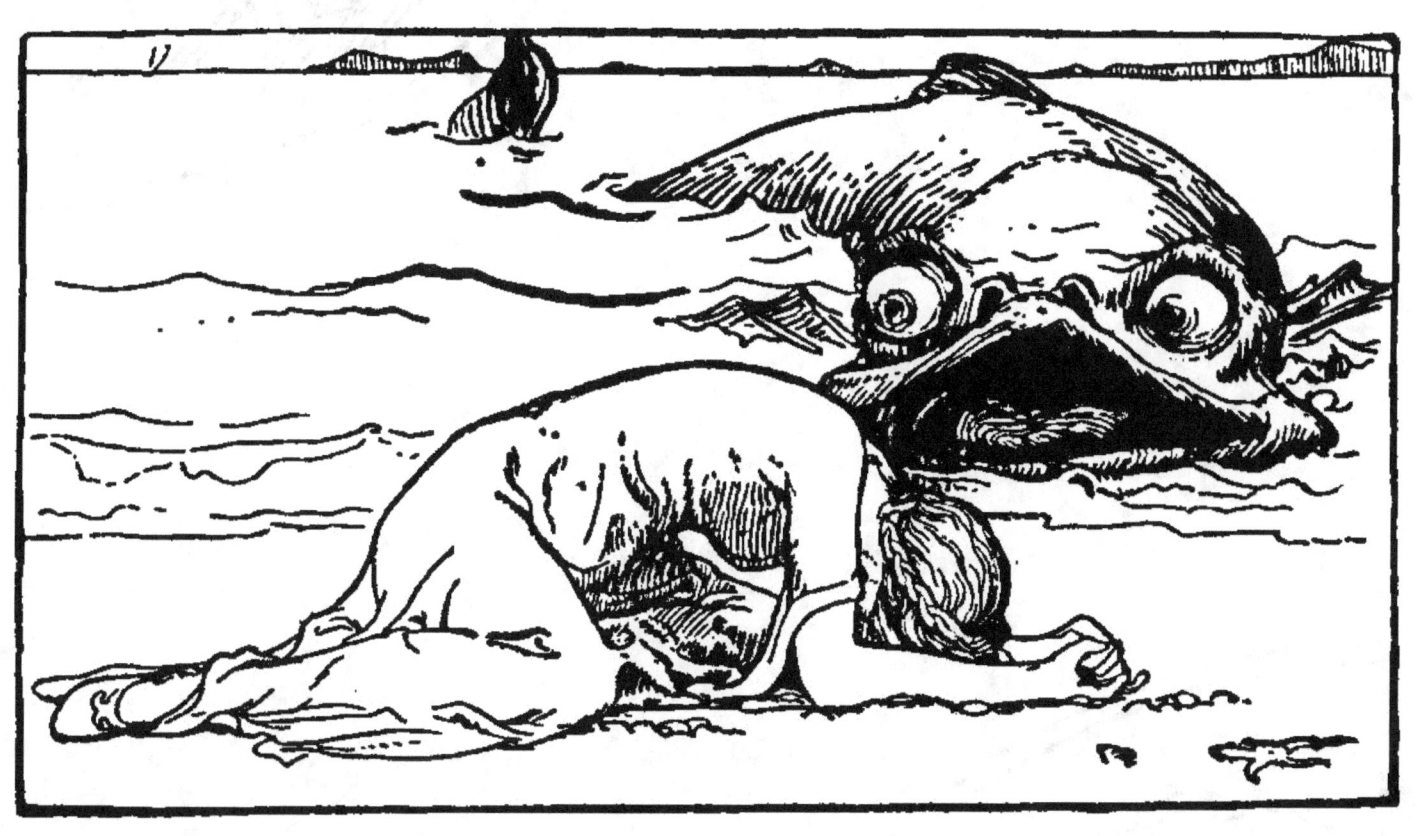

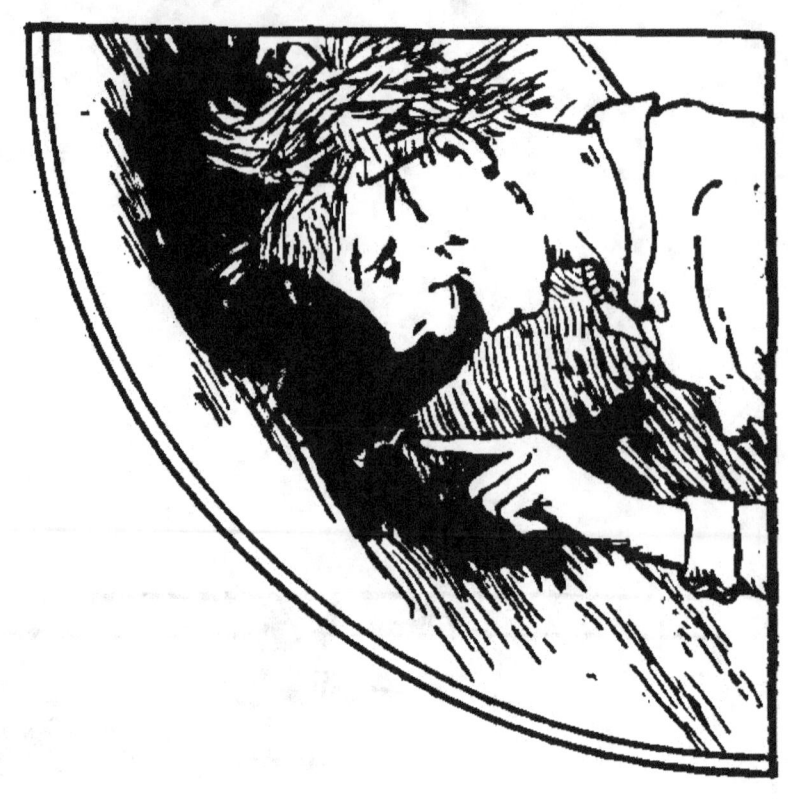

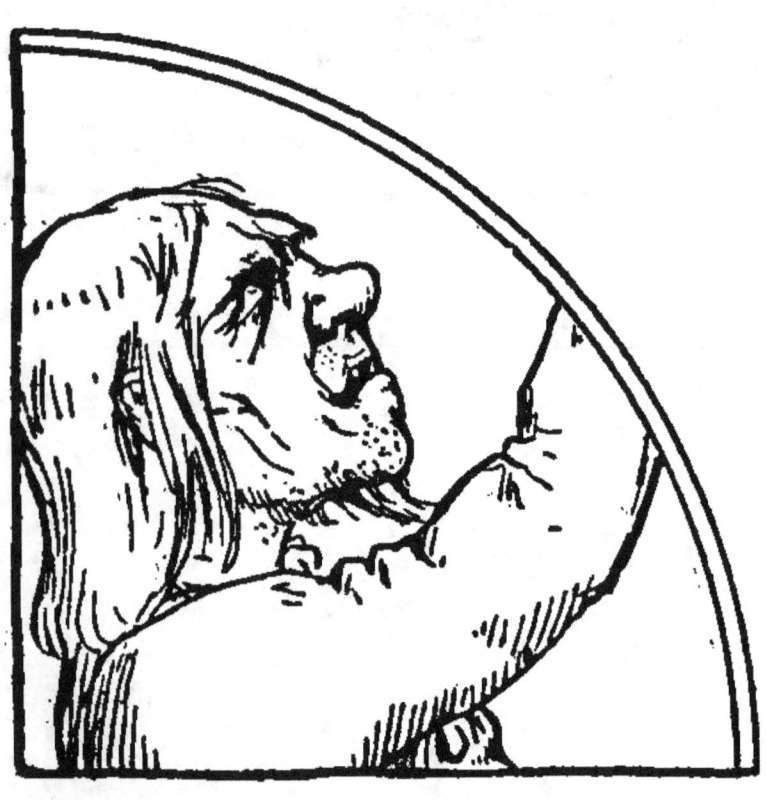

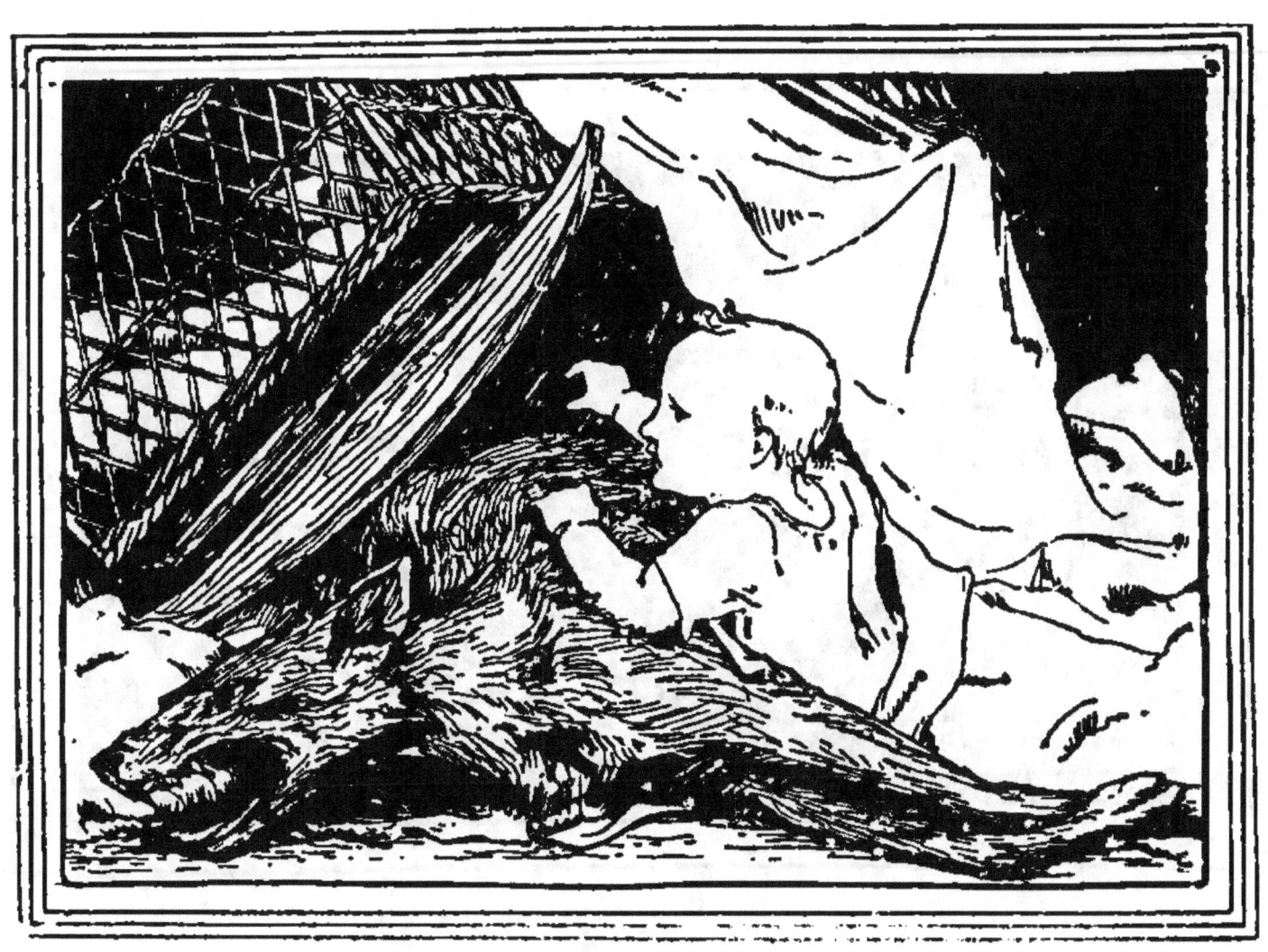

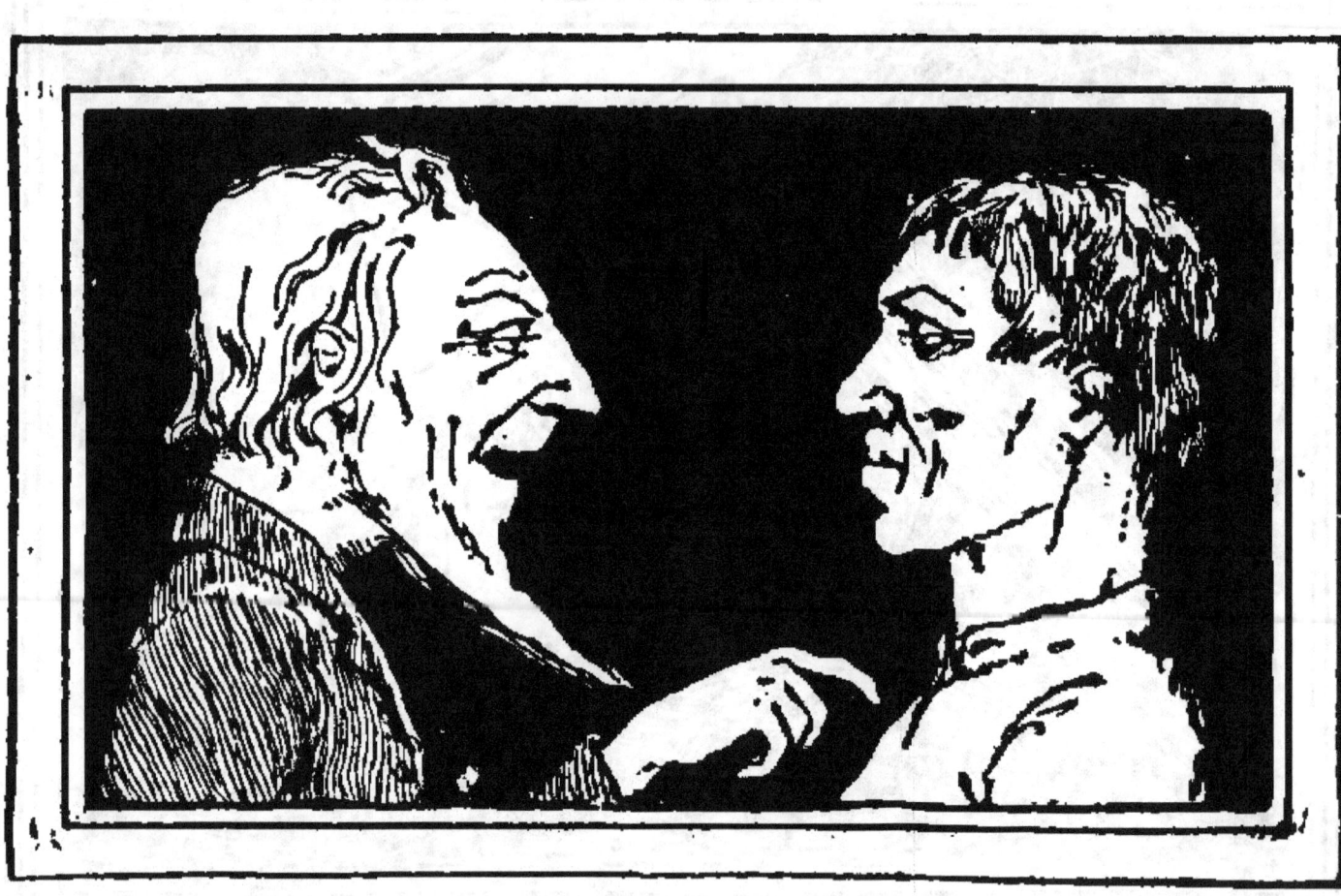

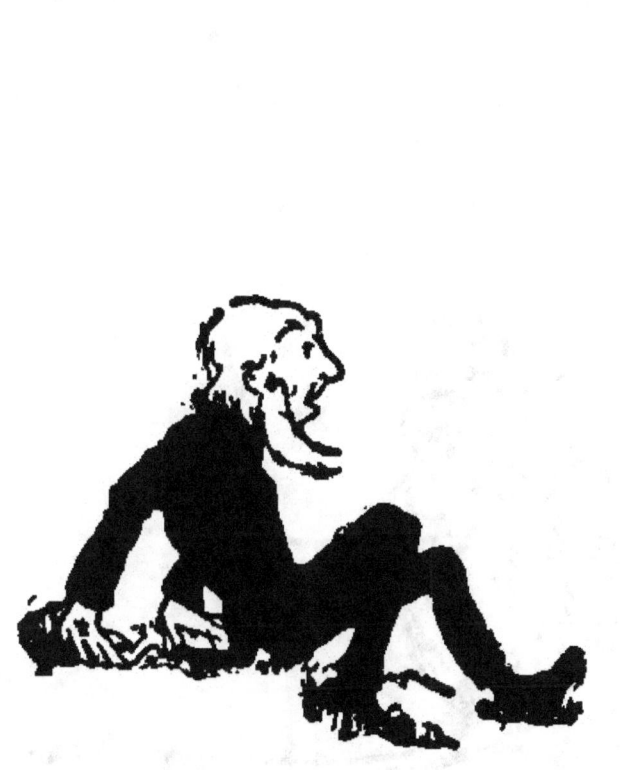
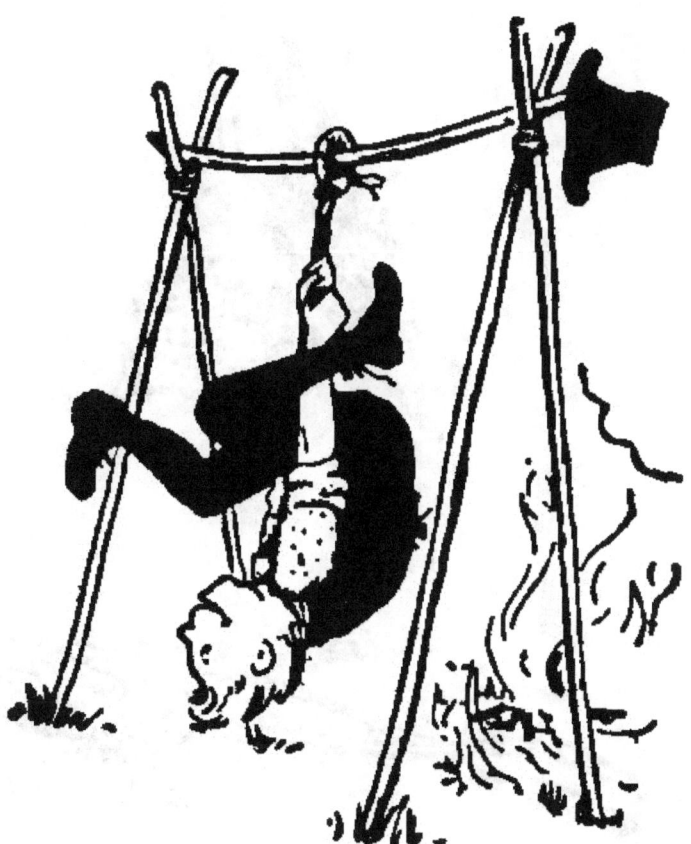

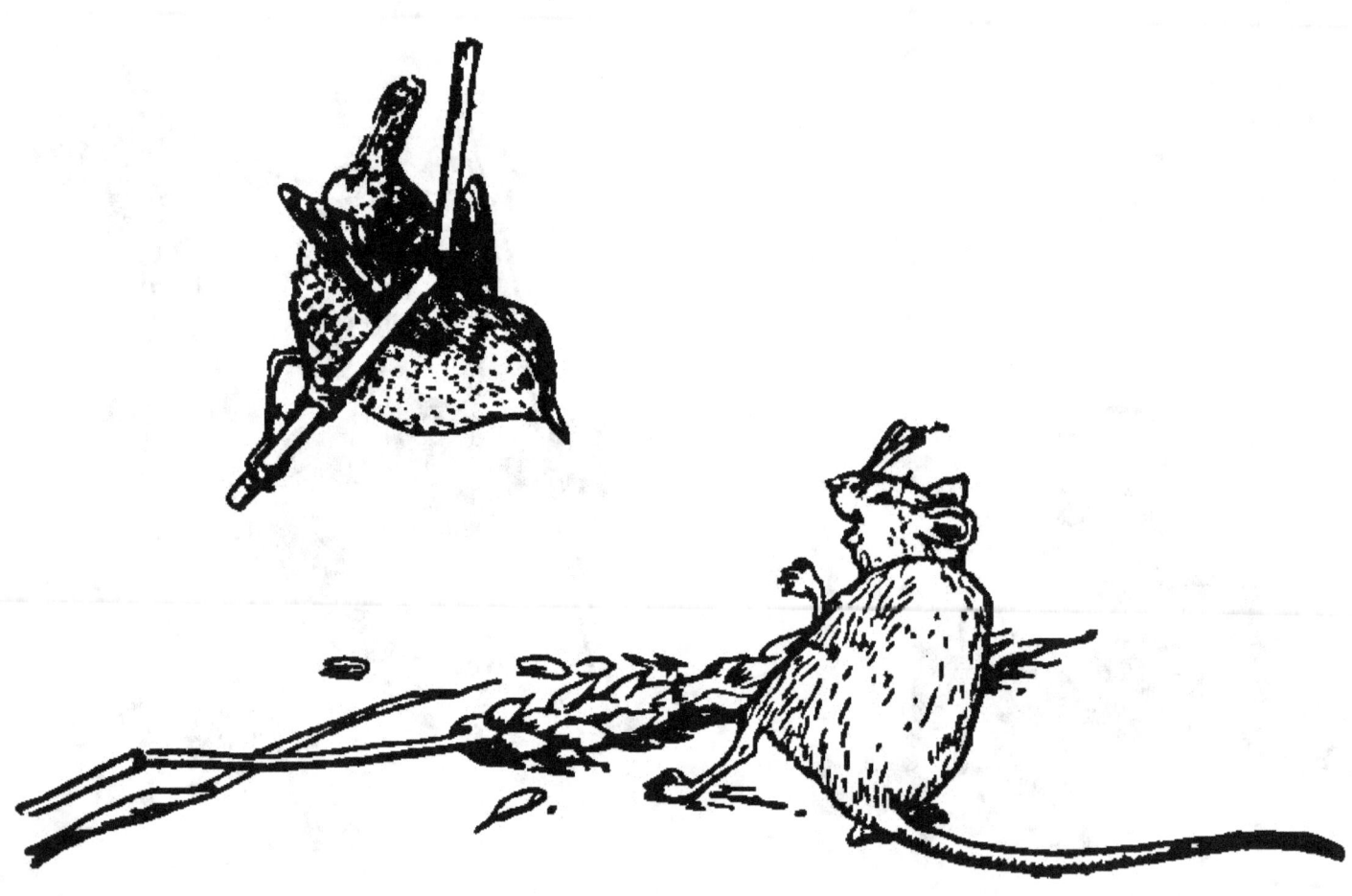

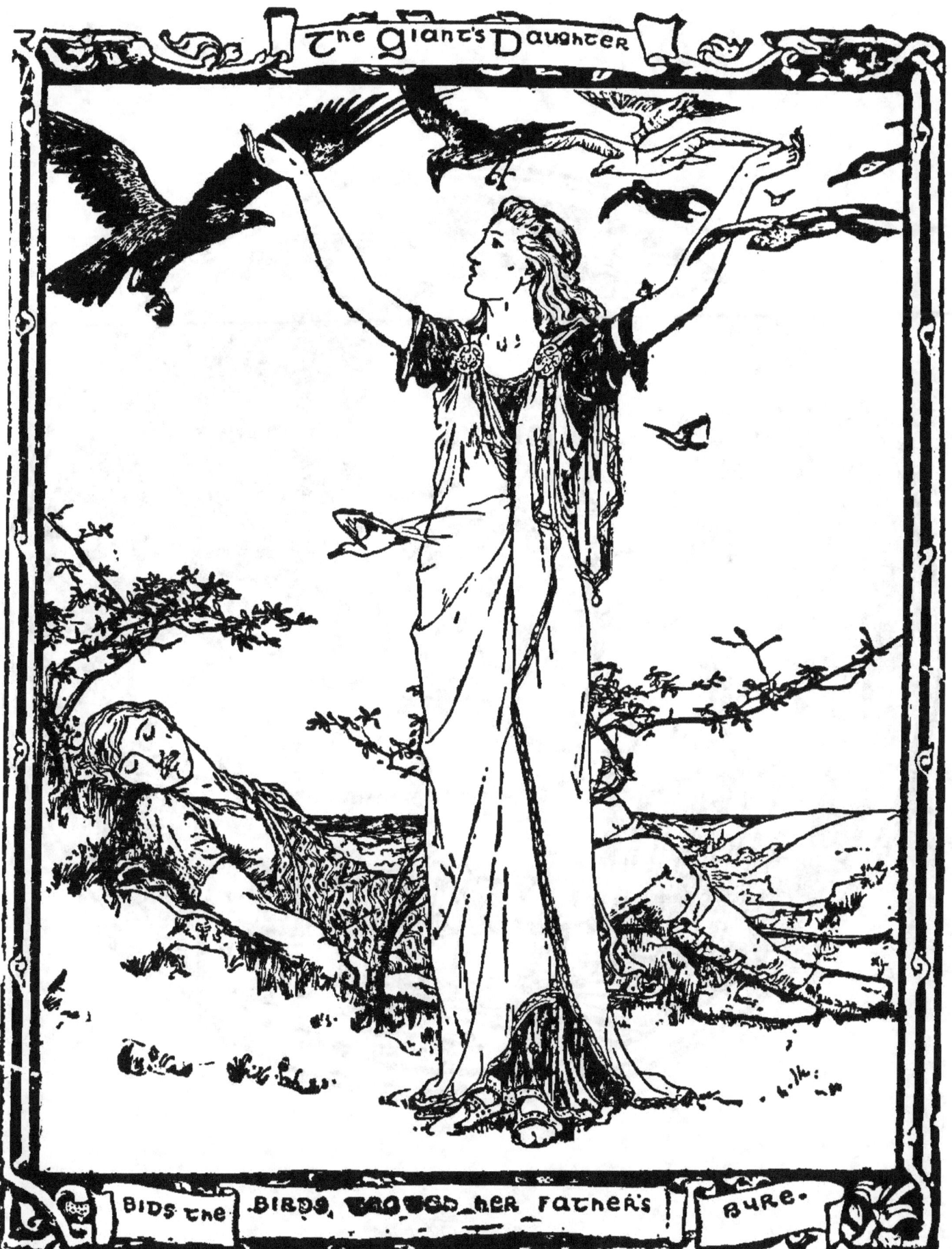

The Giant's Daughter

BIDS THE BIRDS THROUGH HER FATHER'S BYRE.

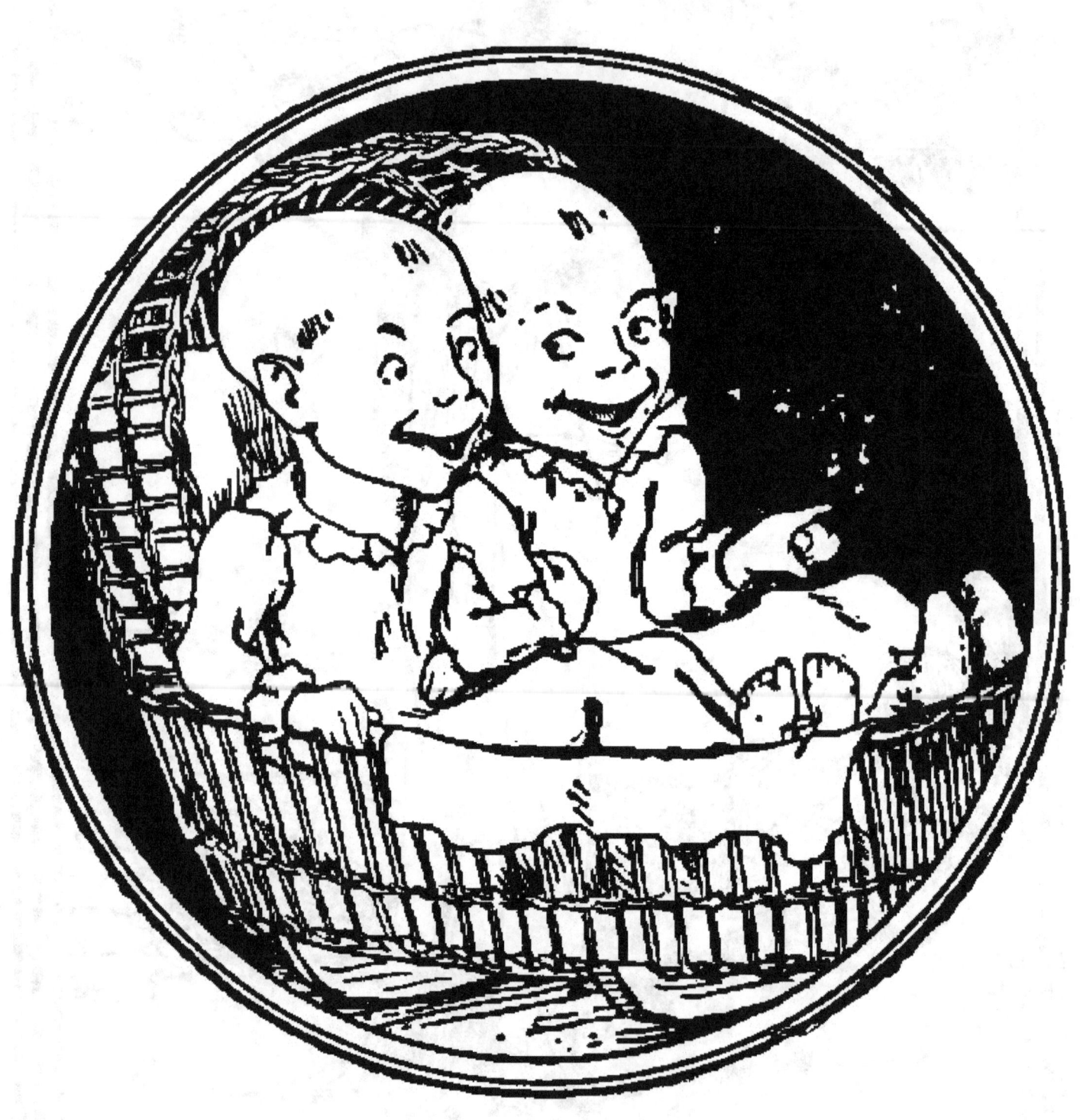

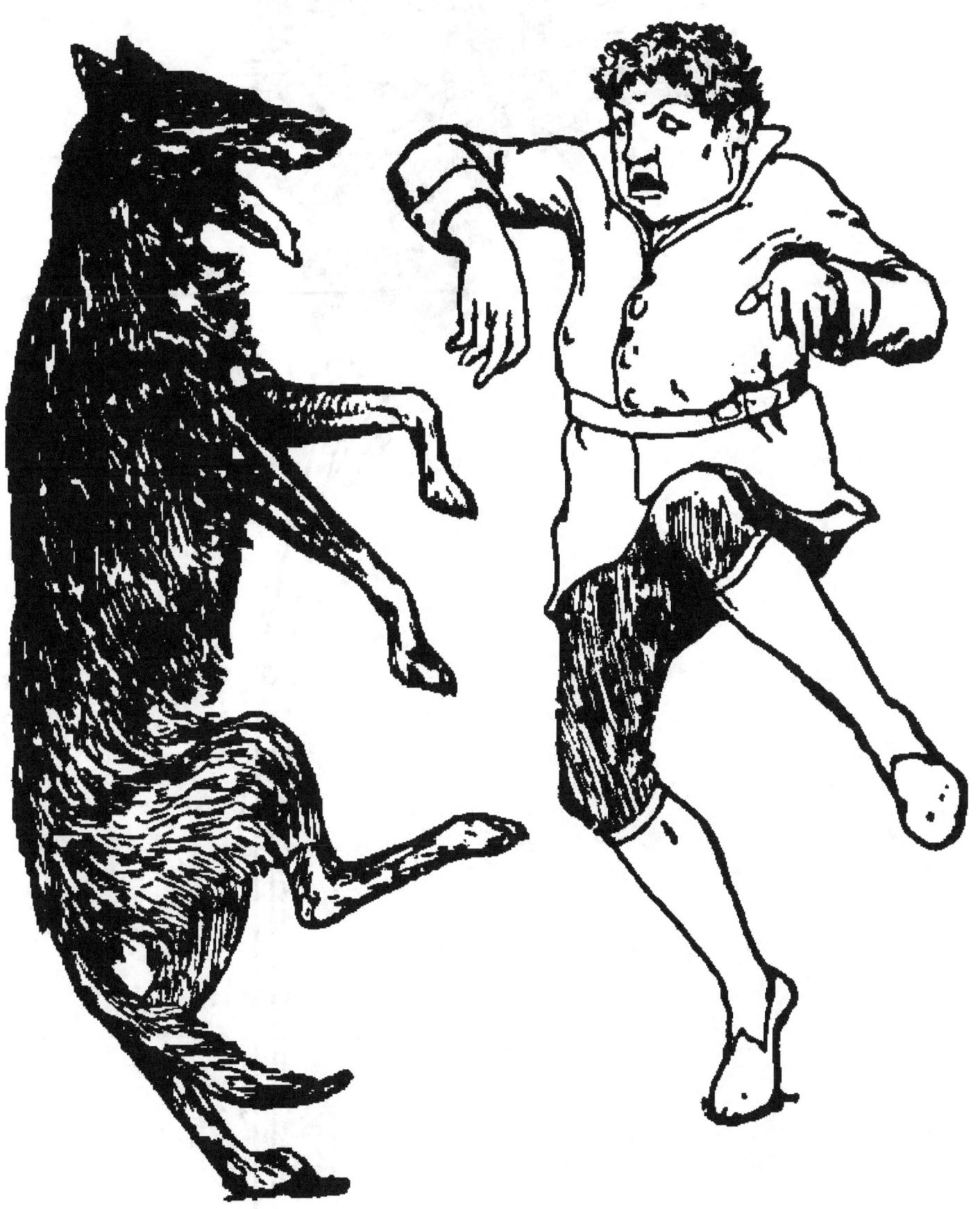

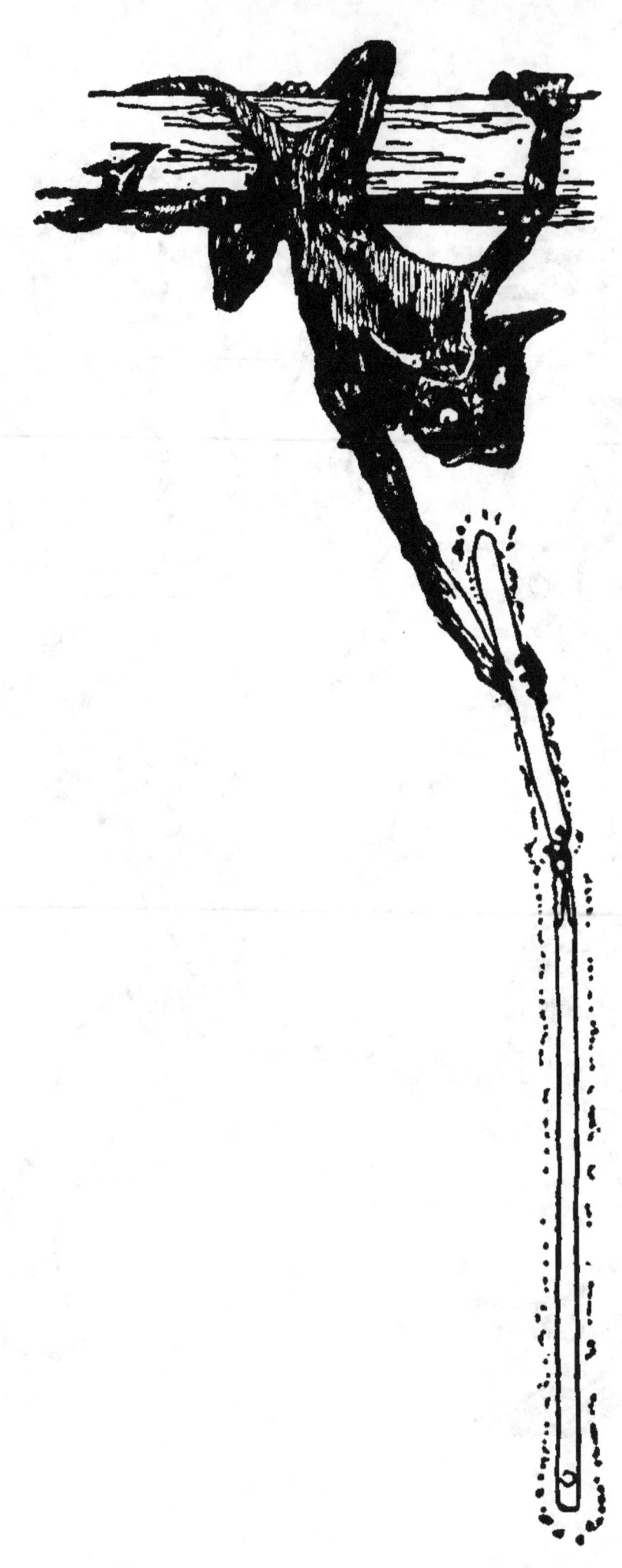

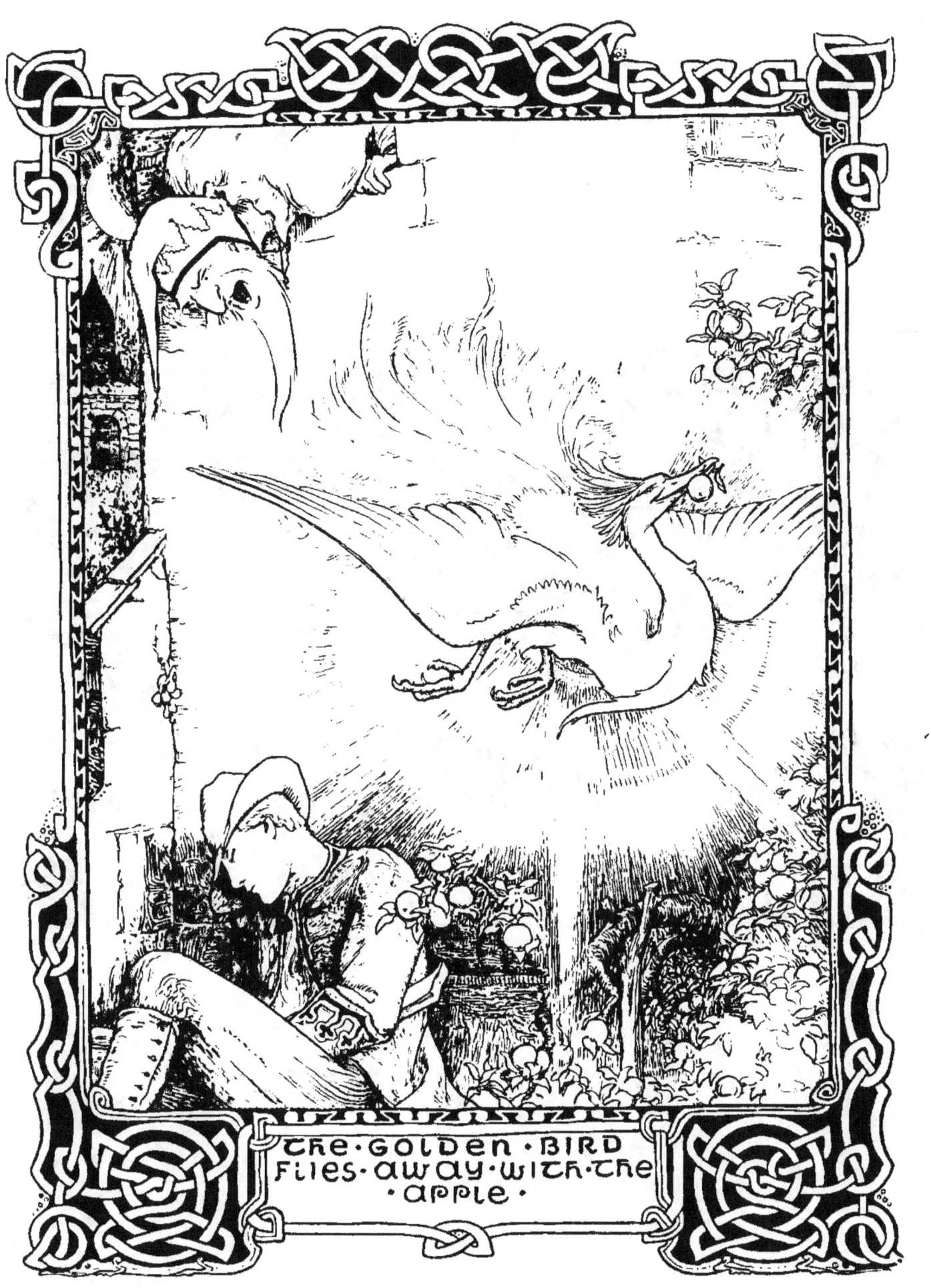

THE·GOLDEN·BIRD
FLIES·AWAY·WITH·THE
·APPLE·

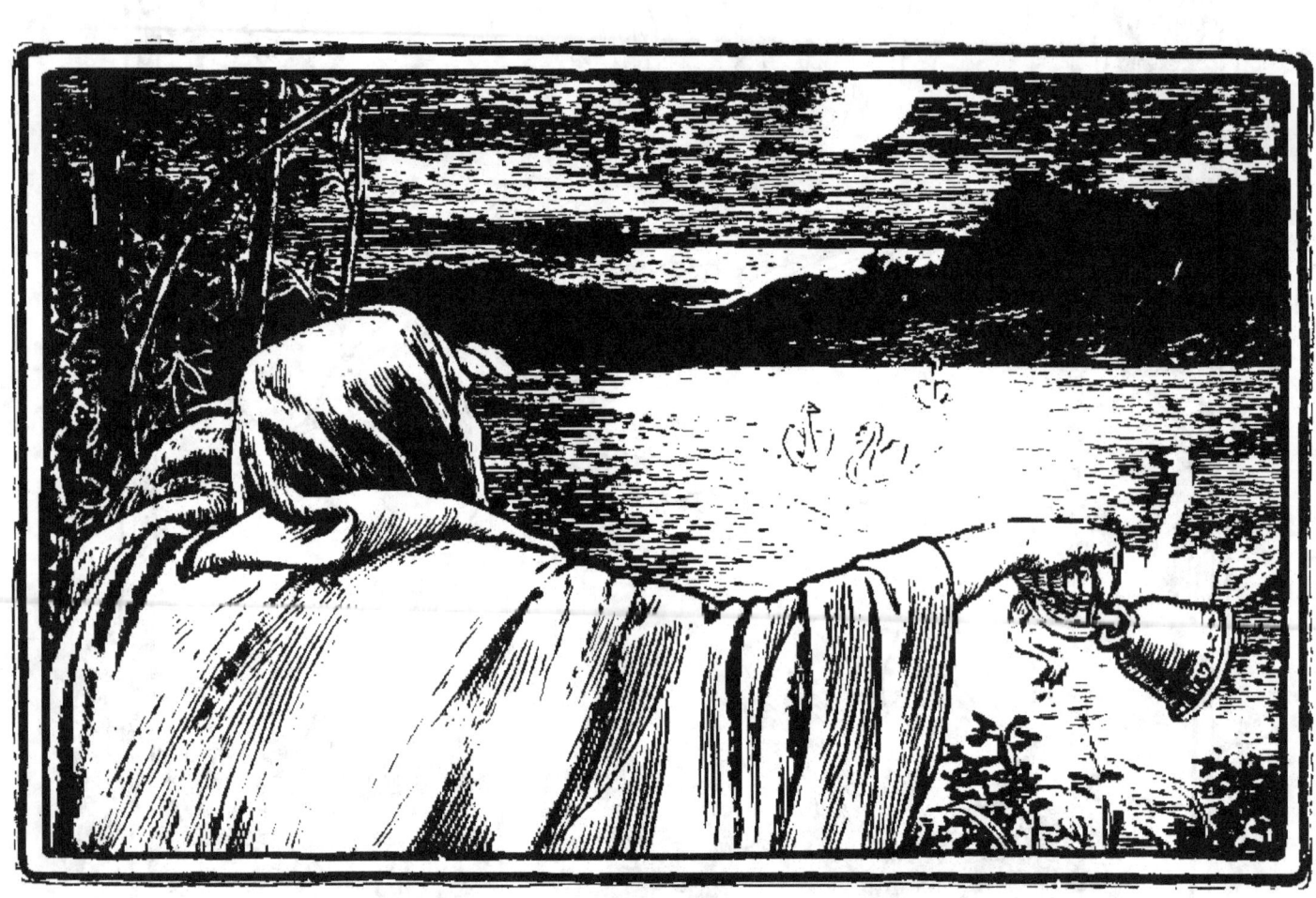

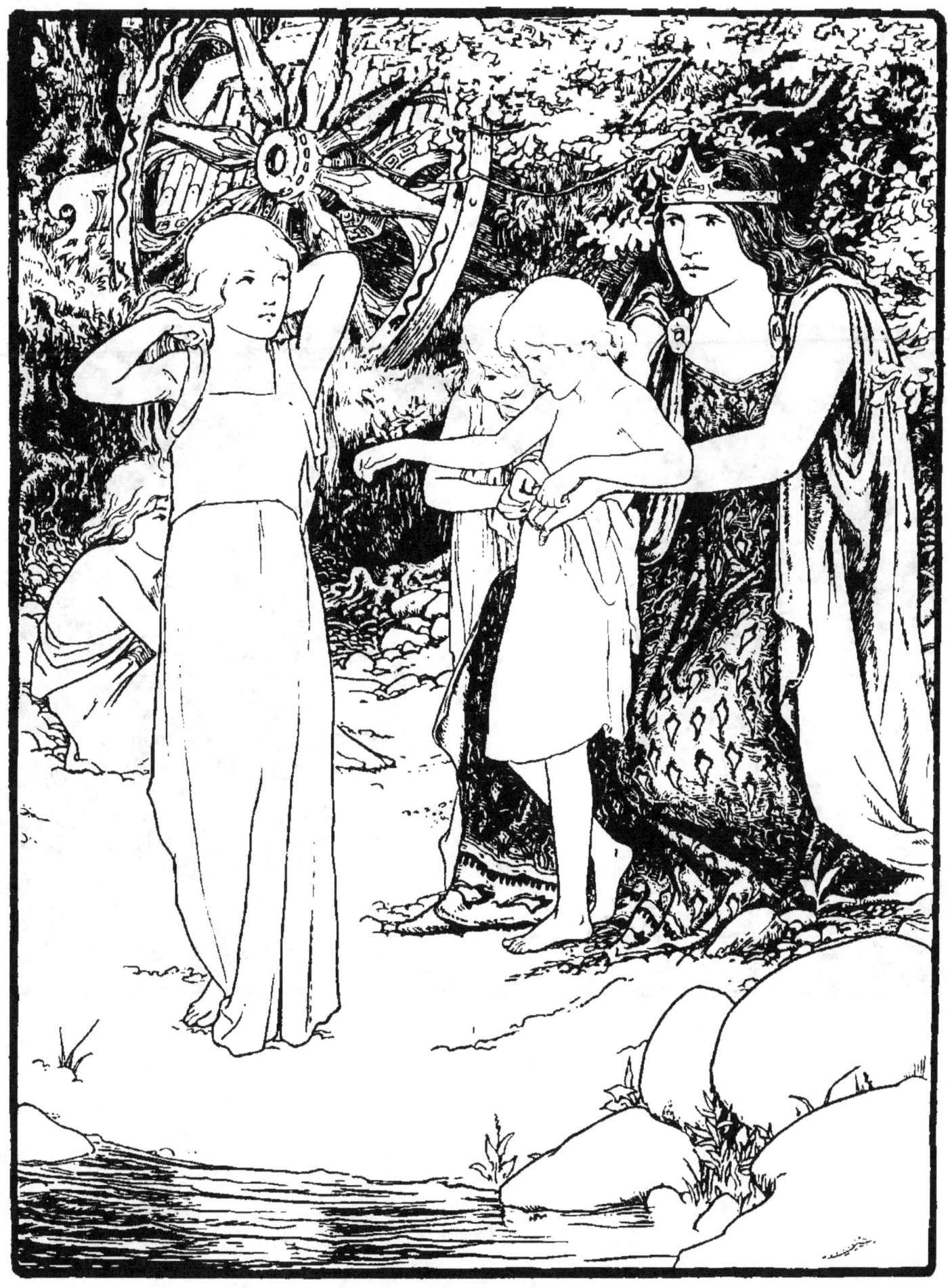

CHILDREN OF LIR

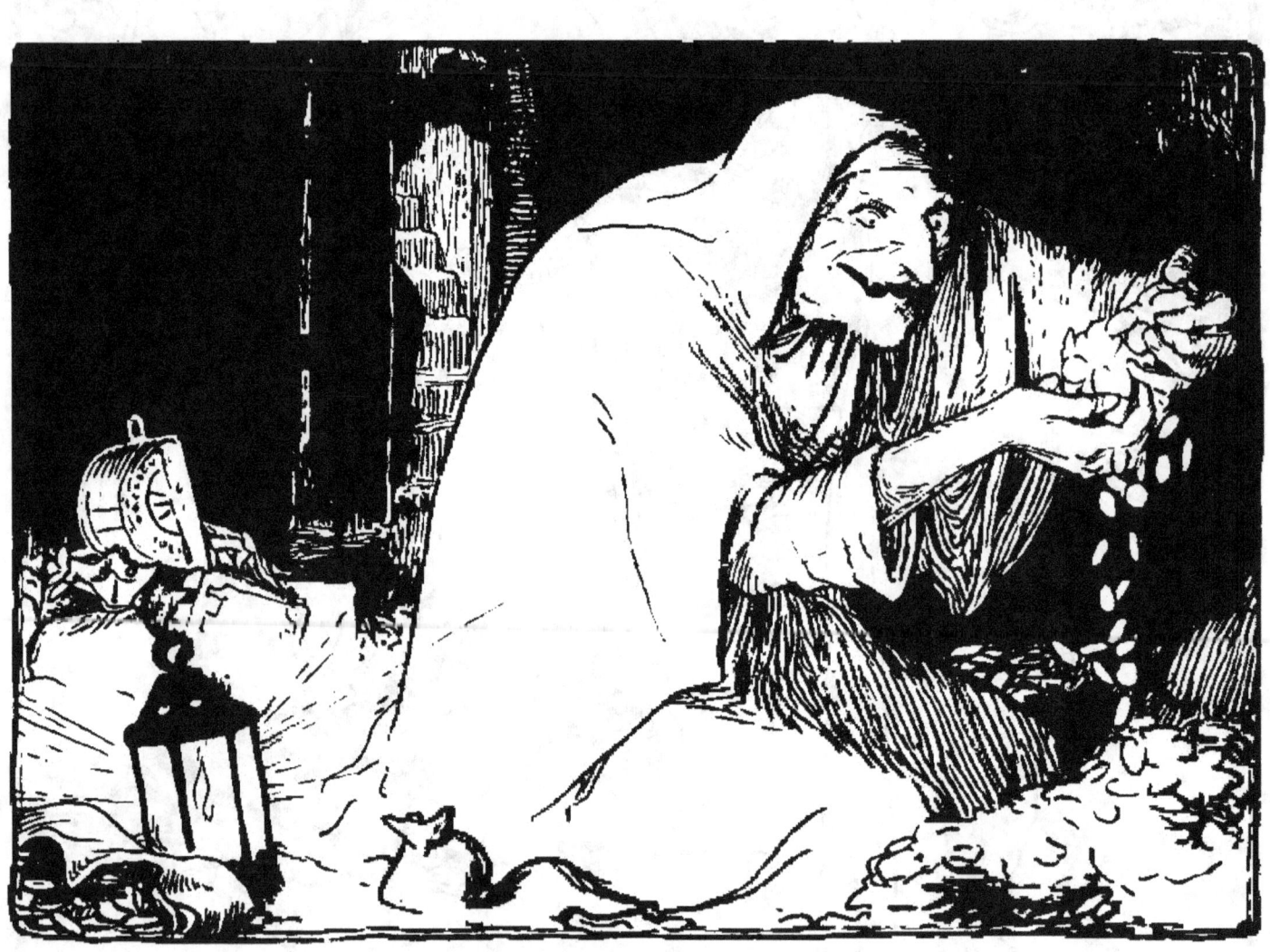

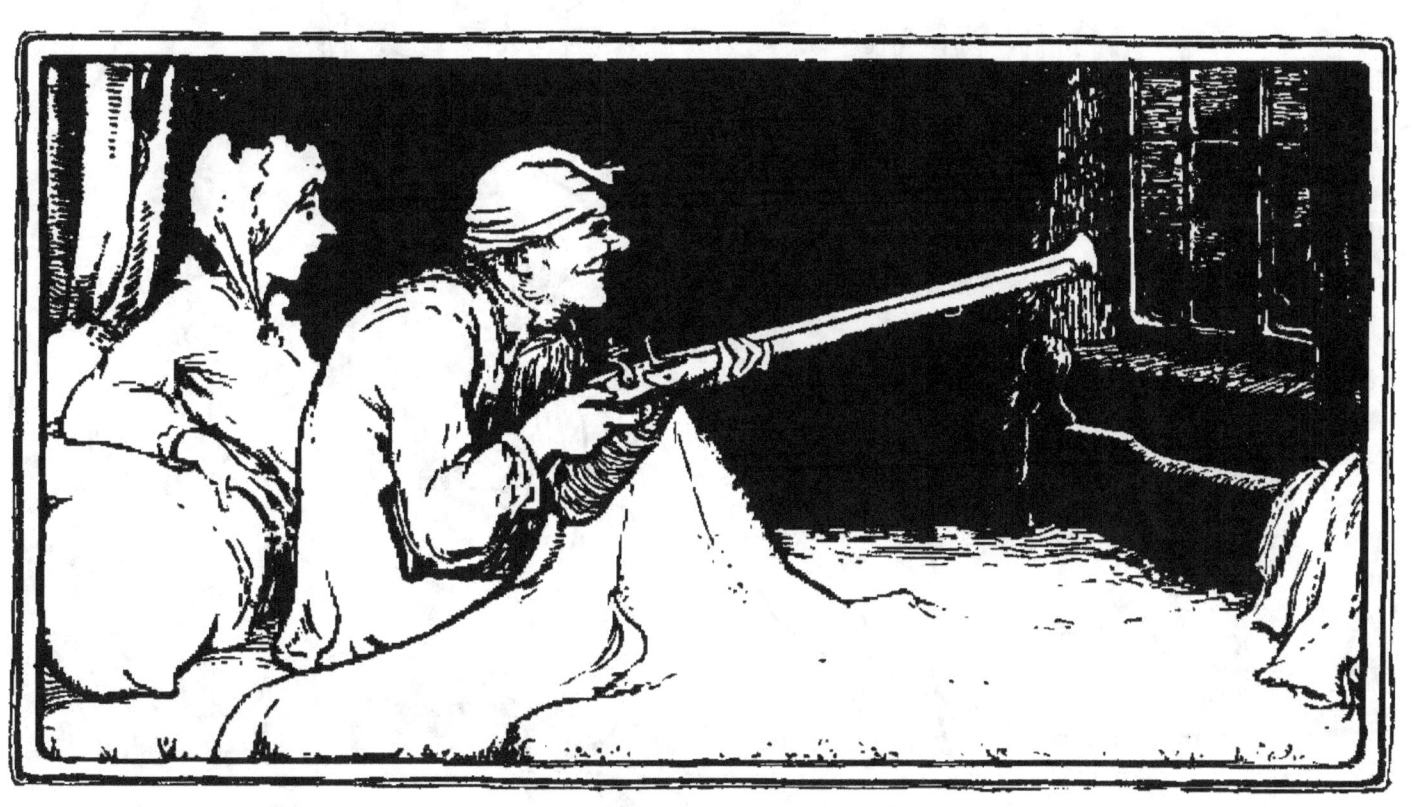

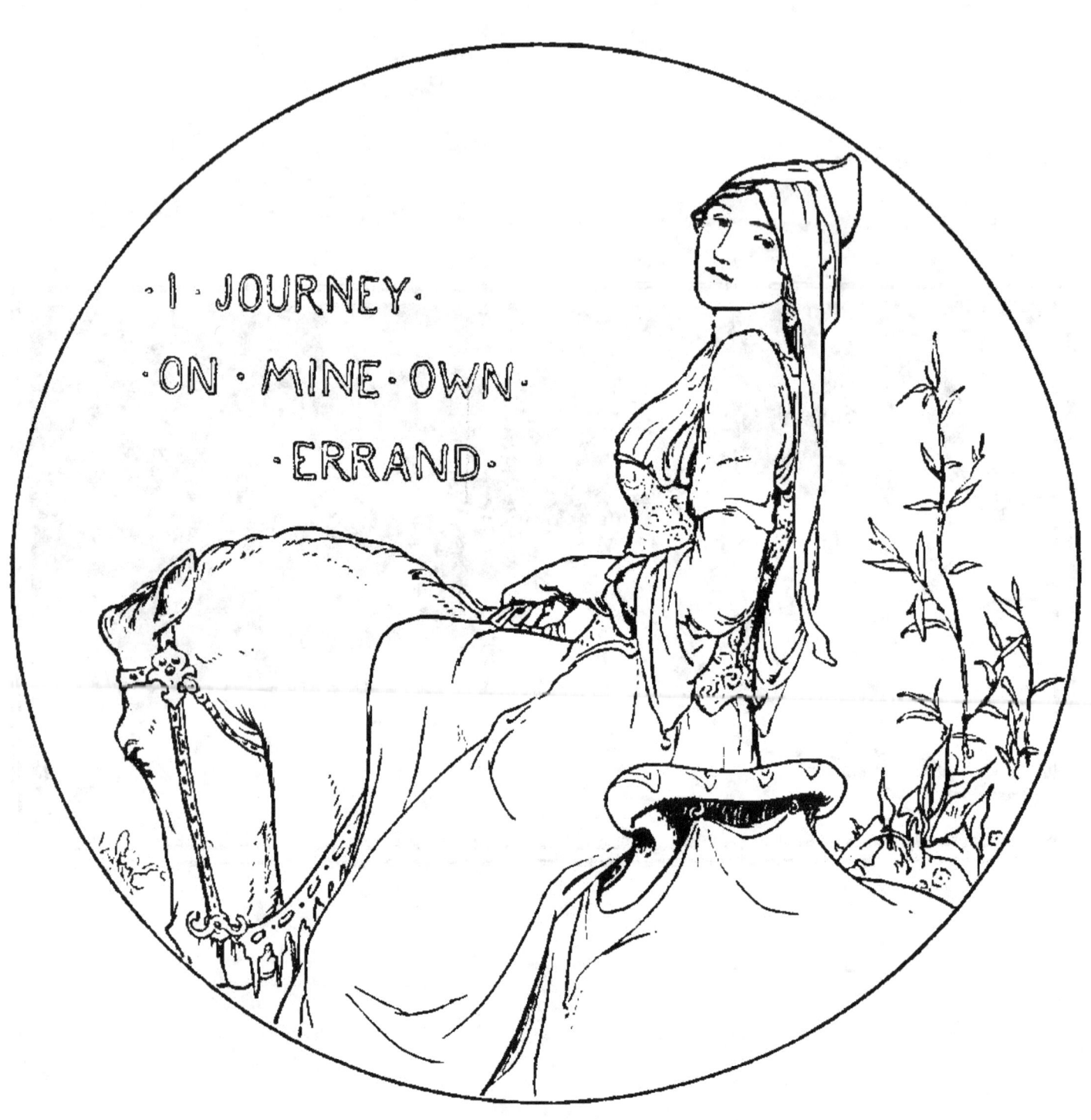

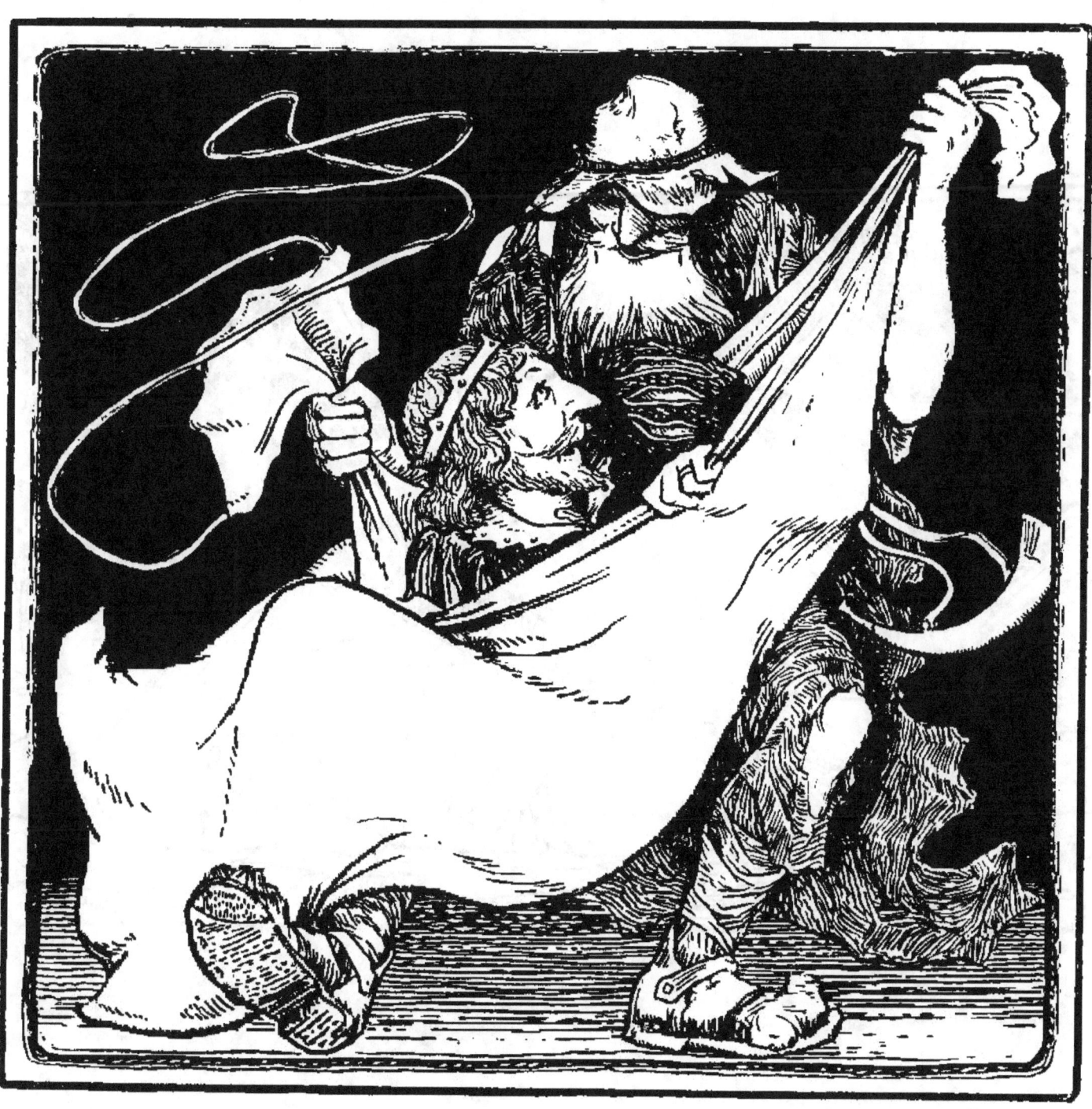

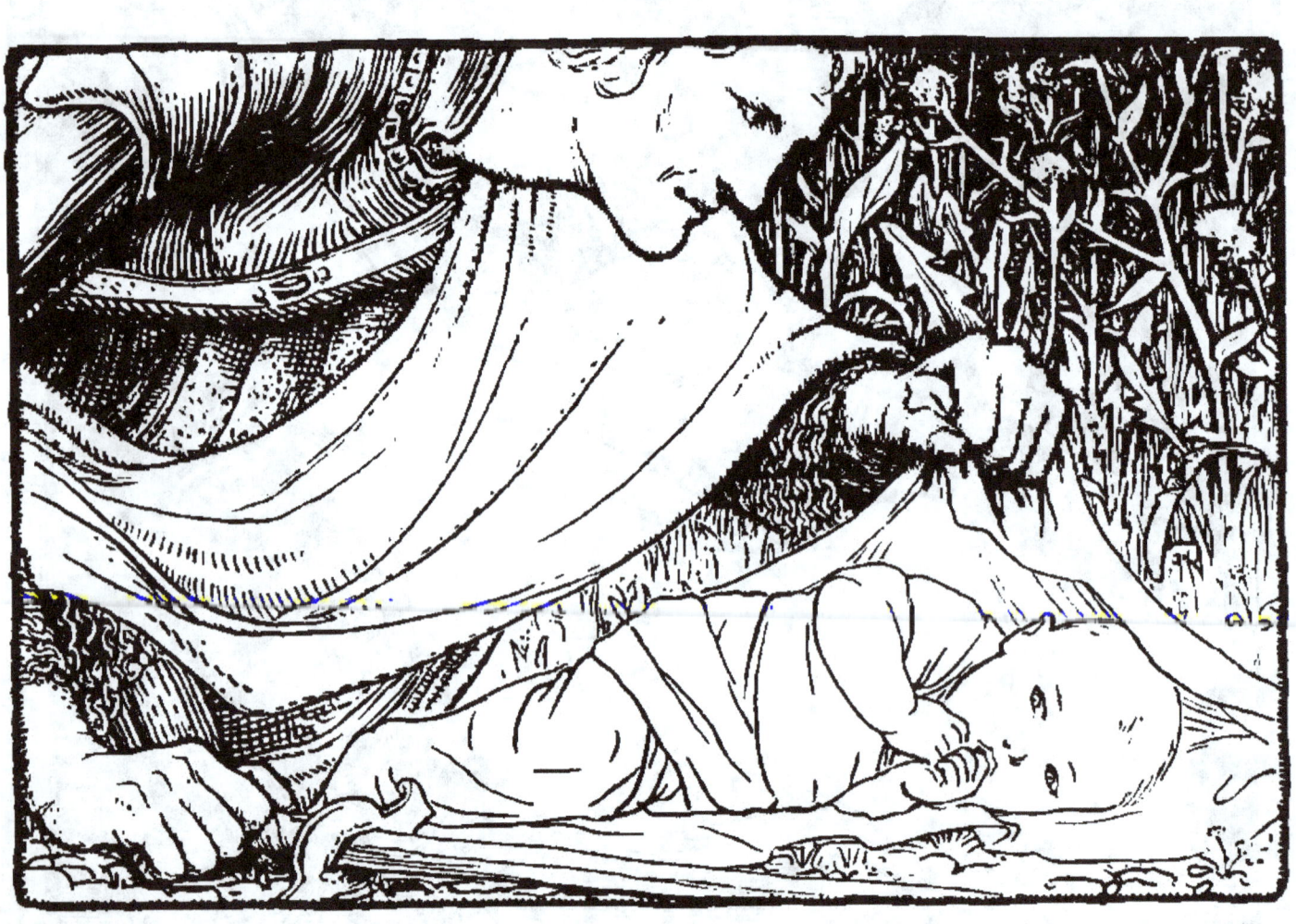

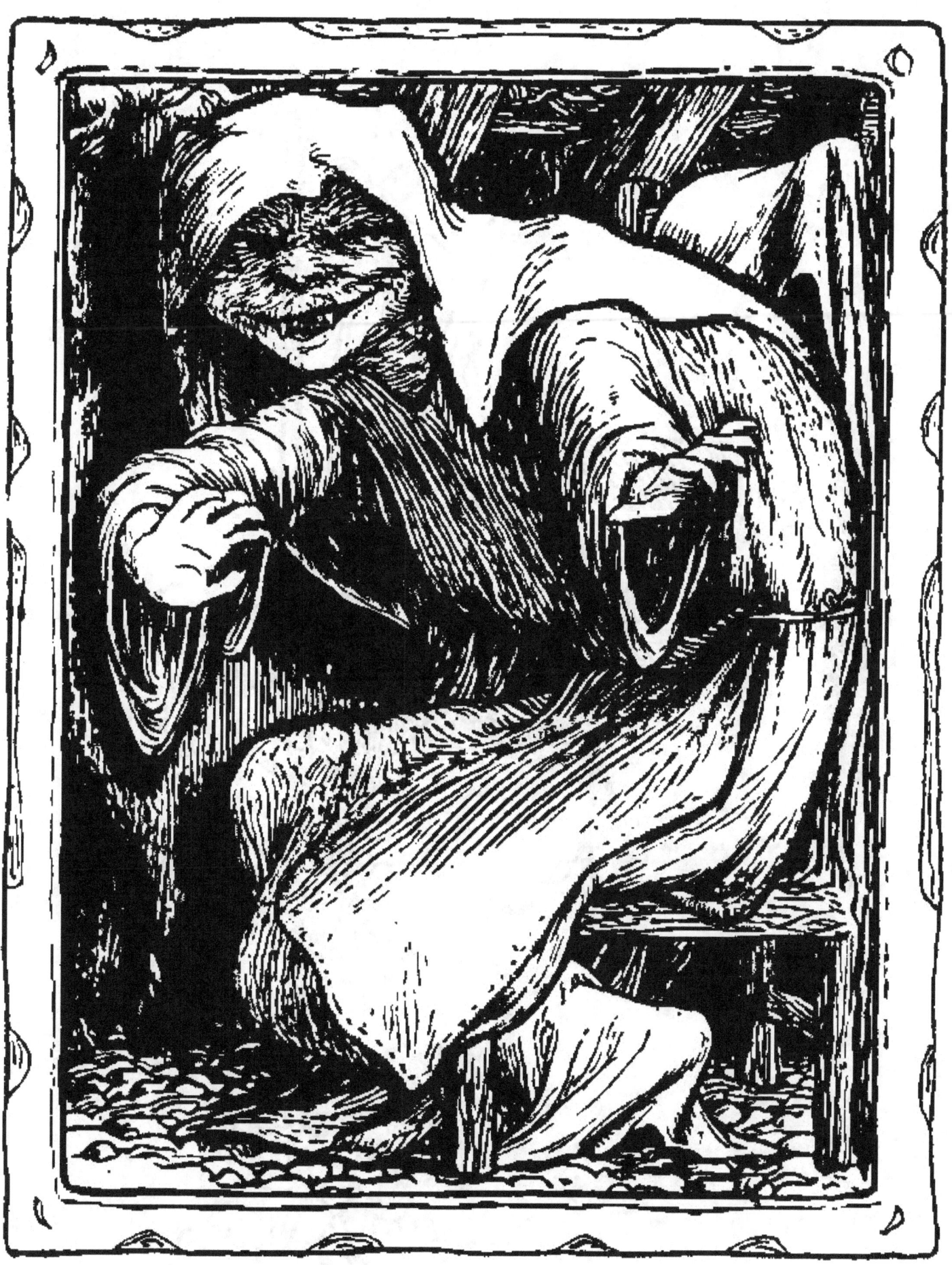

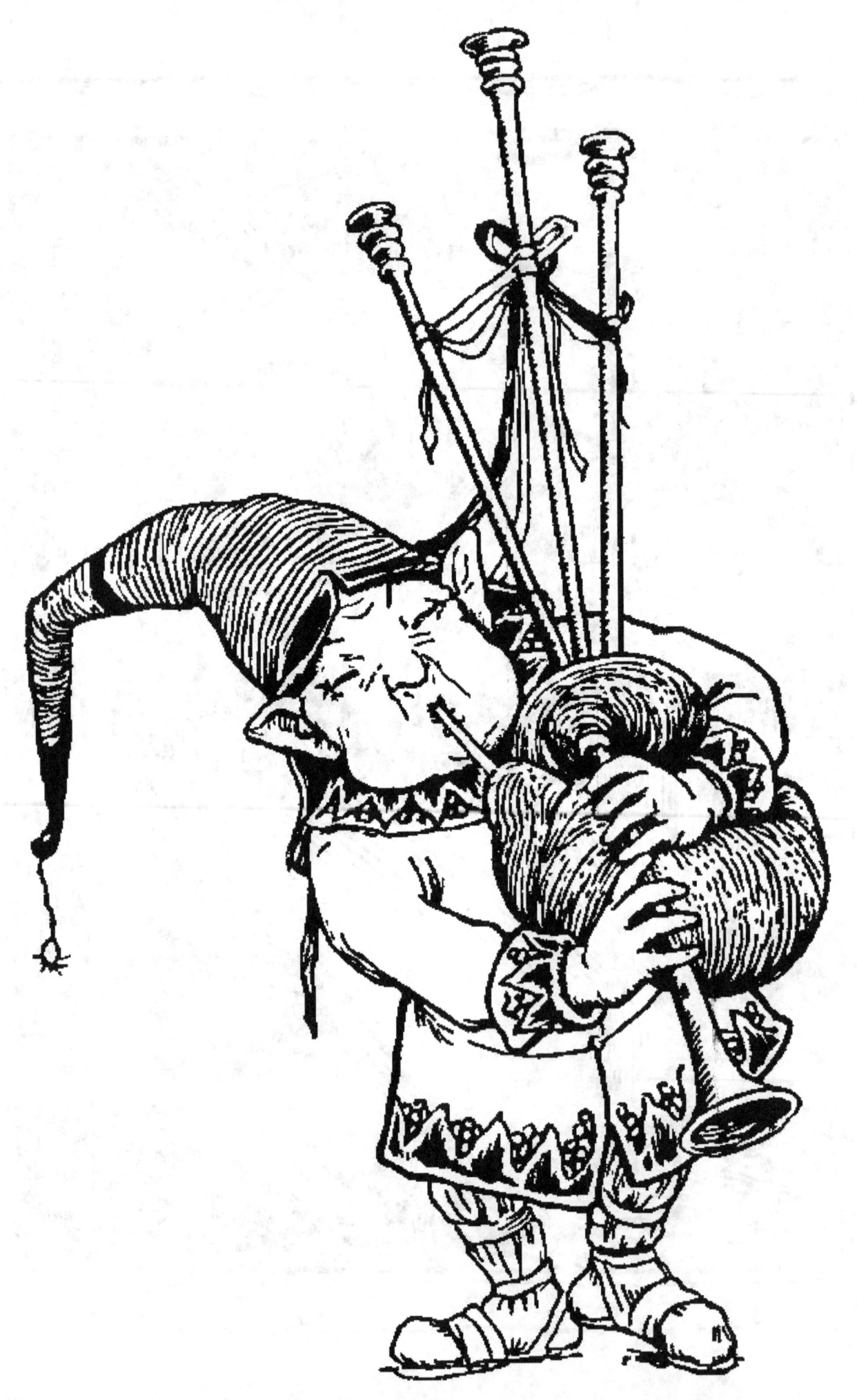

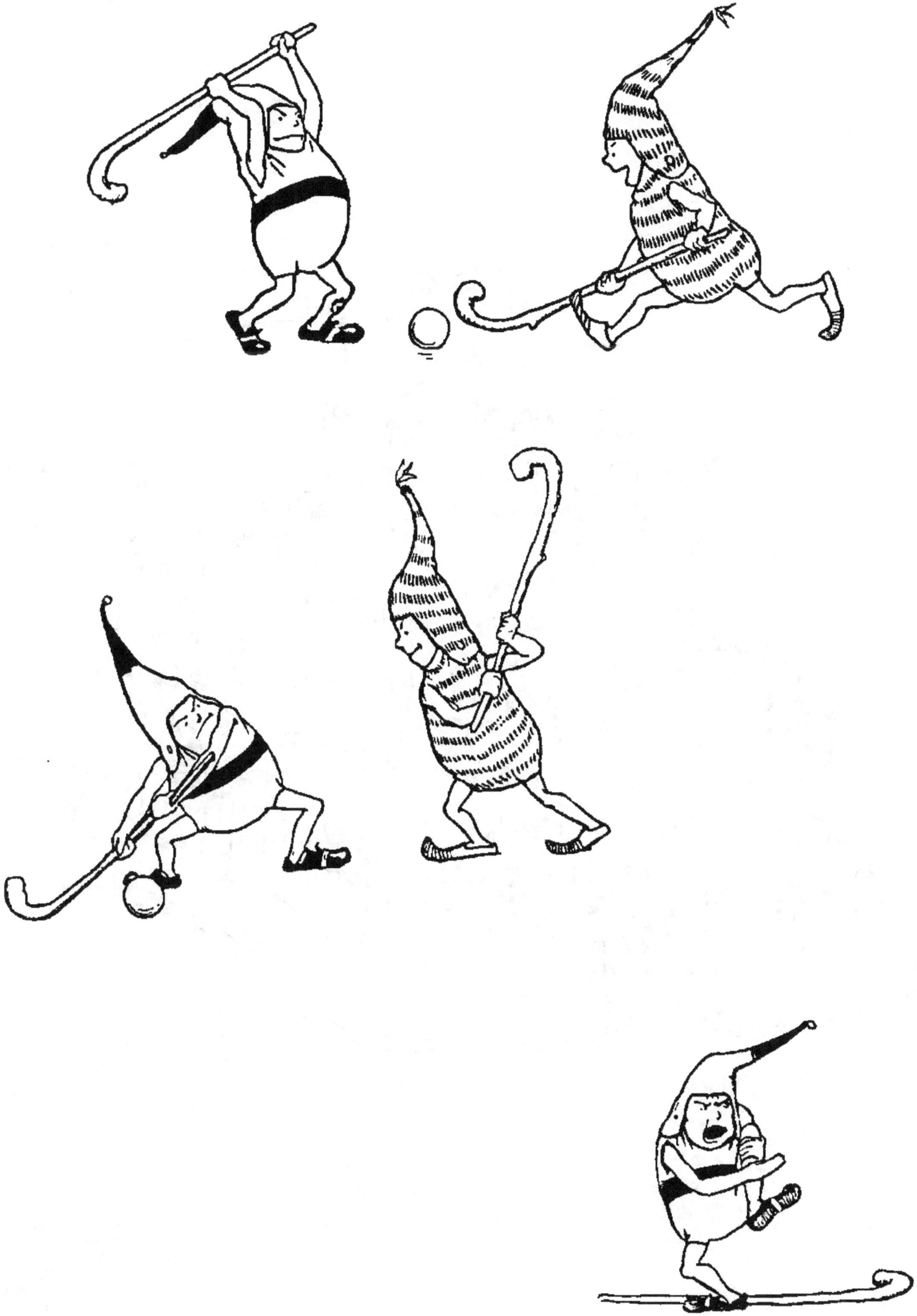

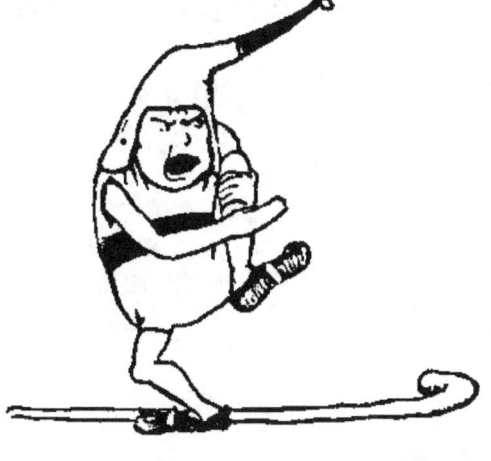

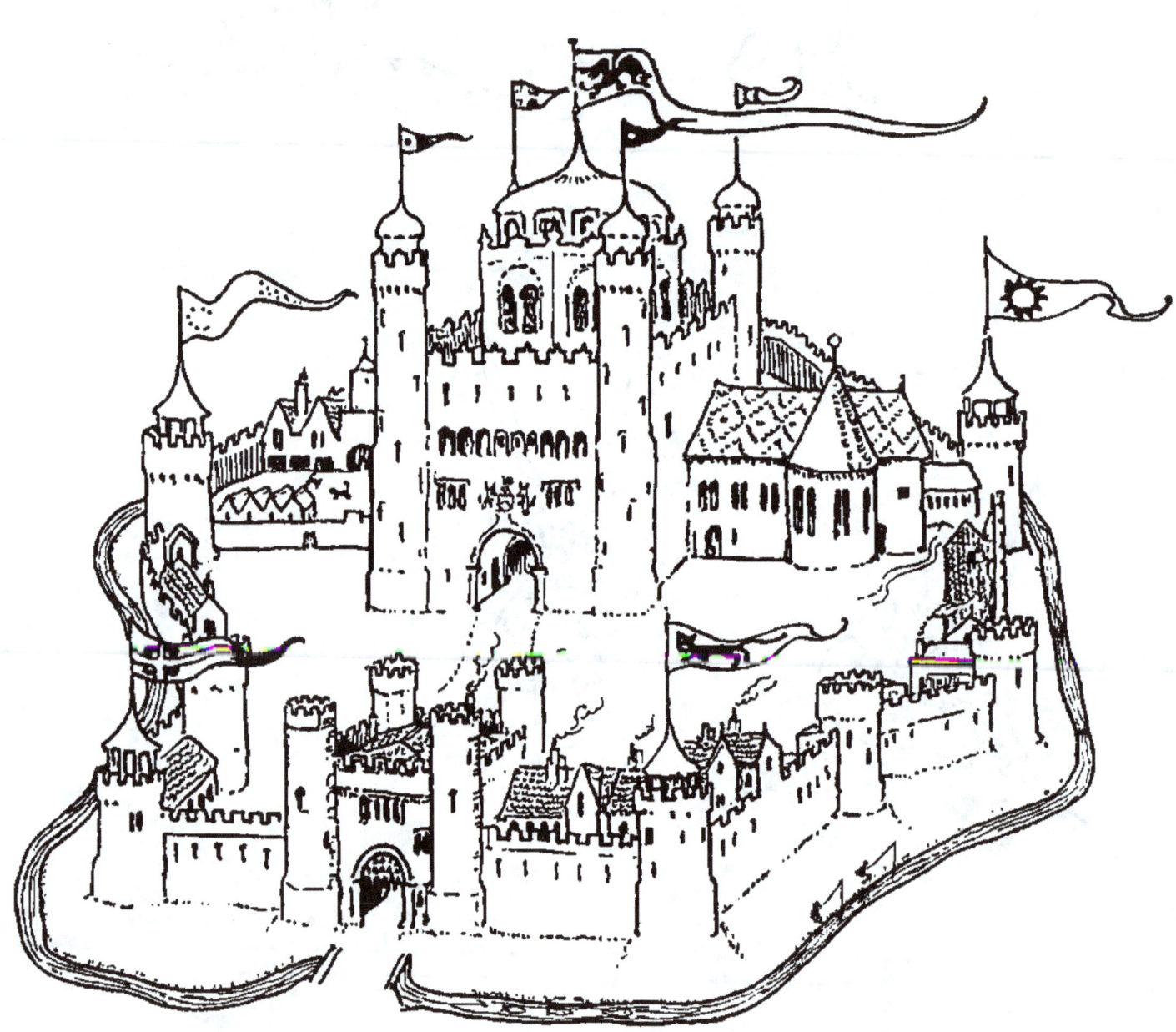

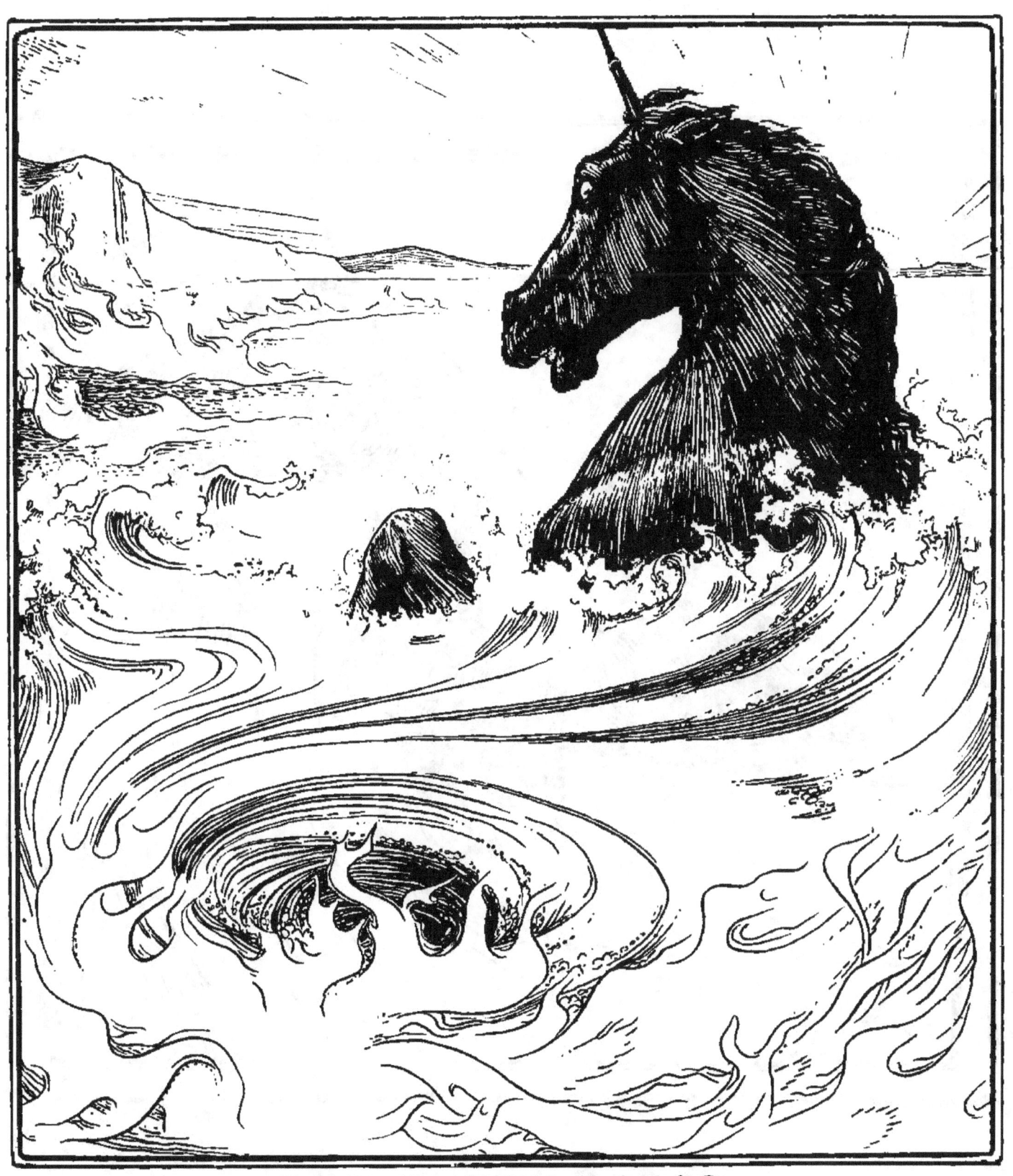

· THE · BLACK · HORSE ·

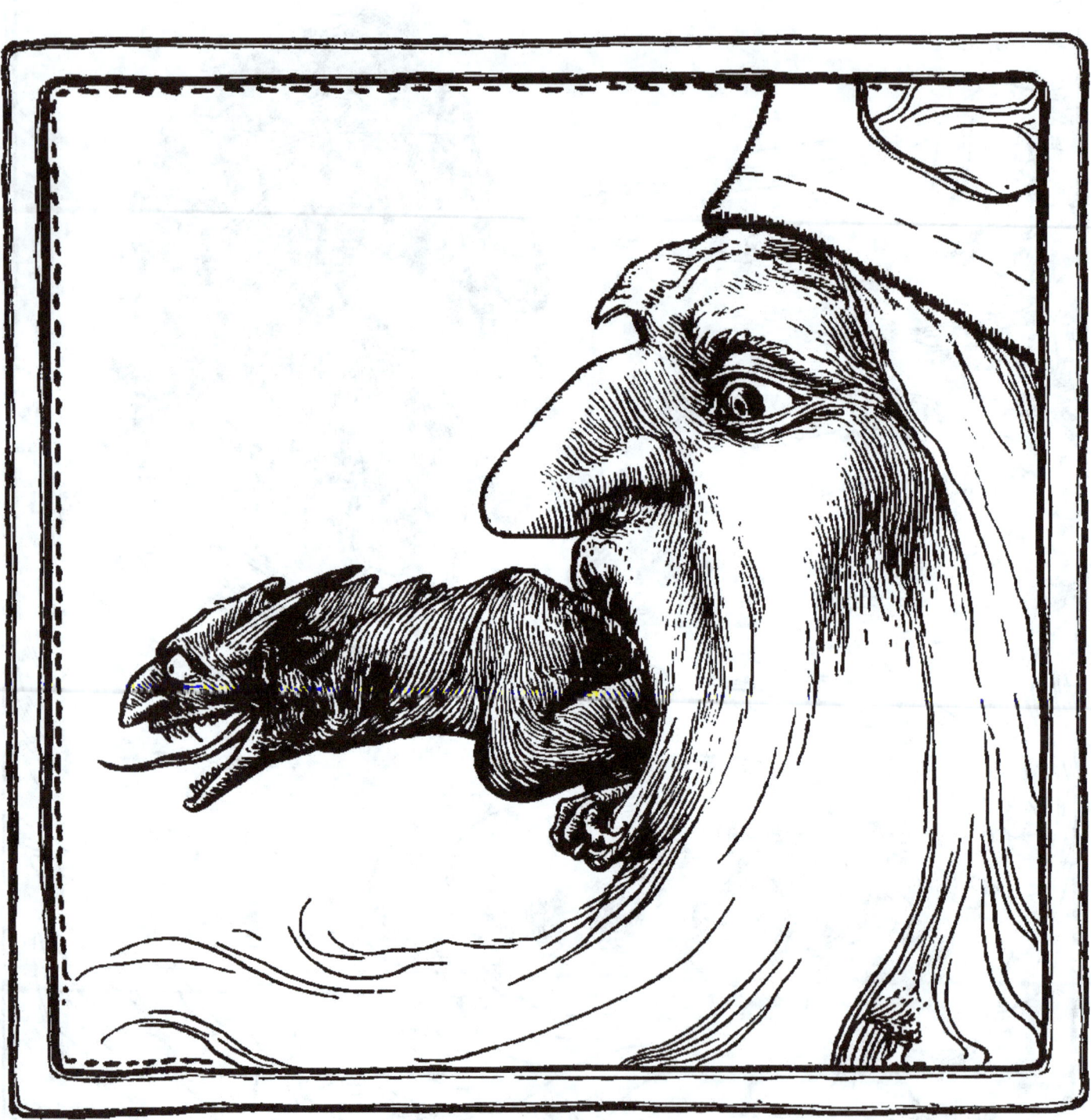

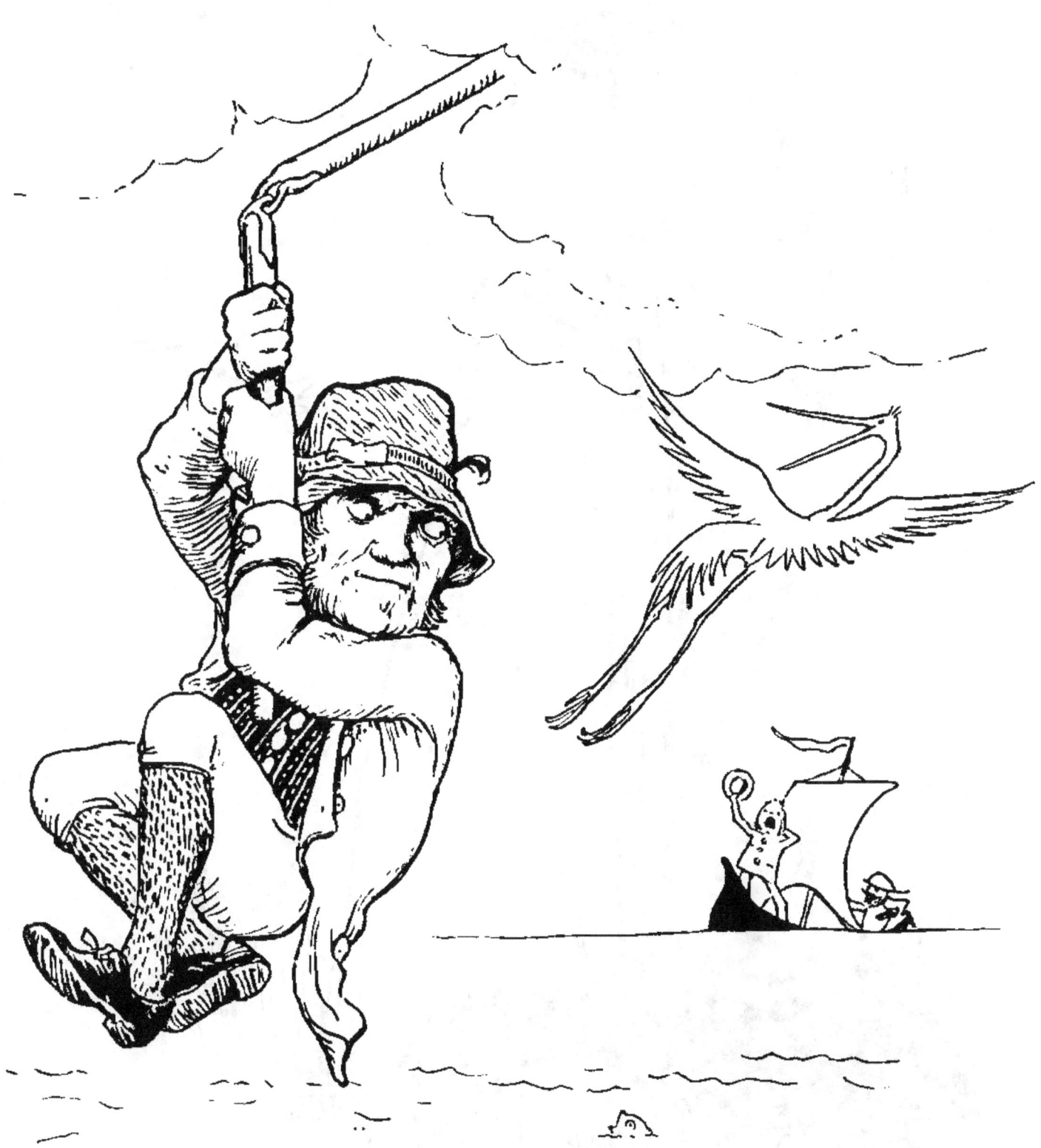

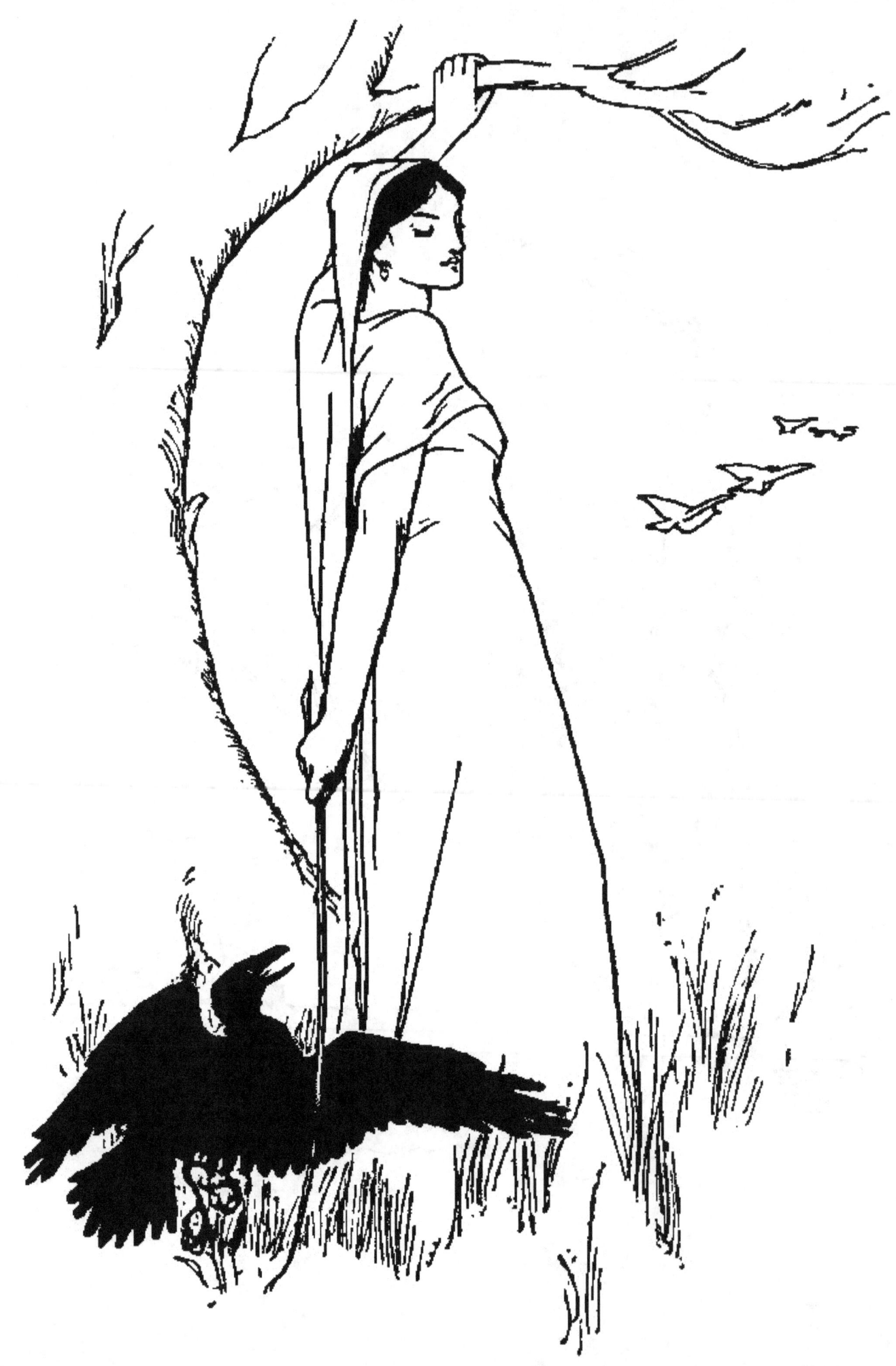

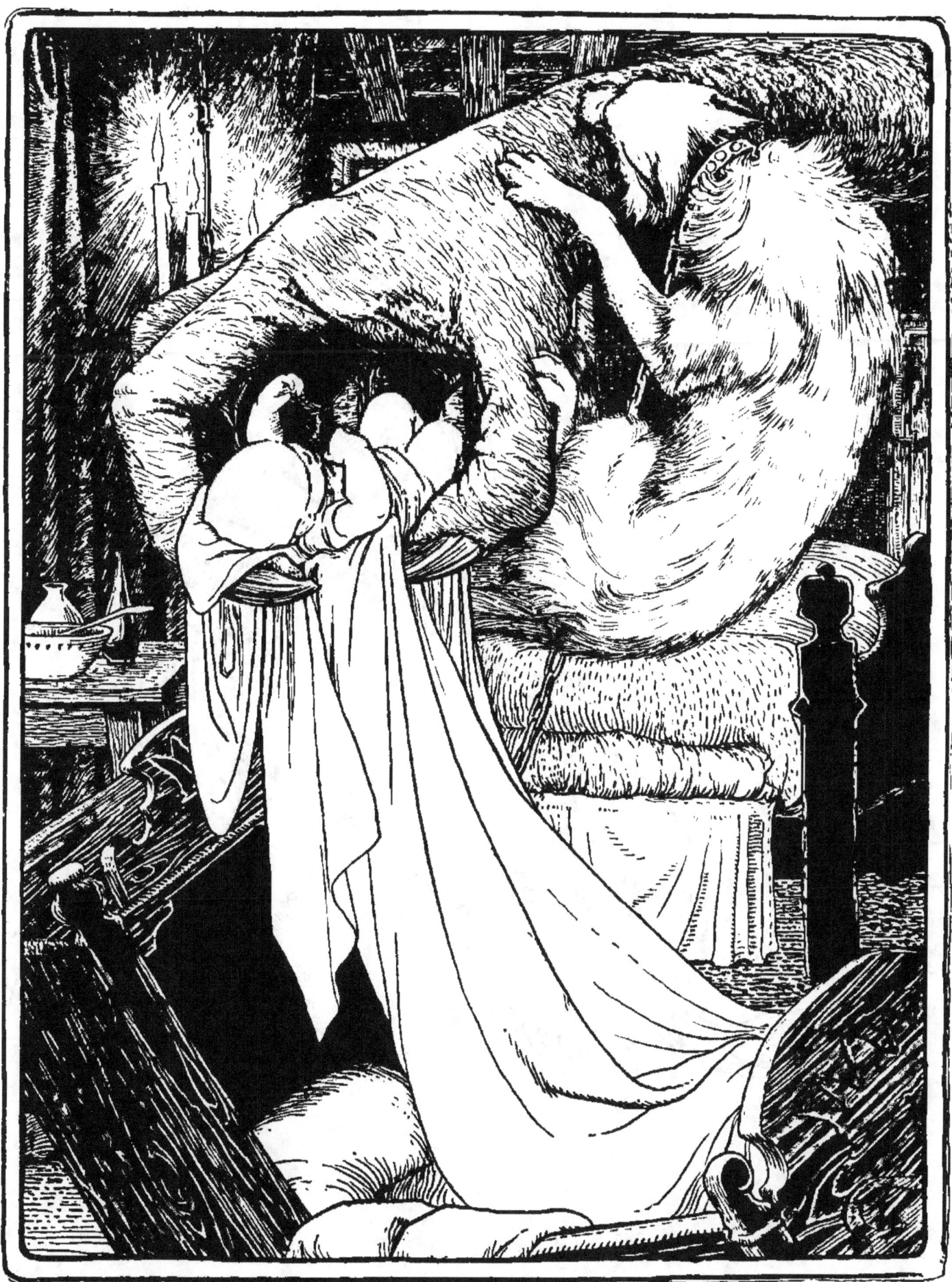

MORRAHA

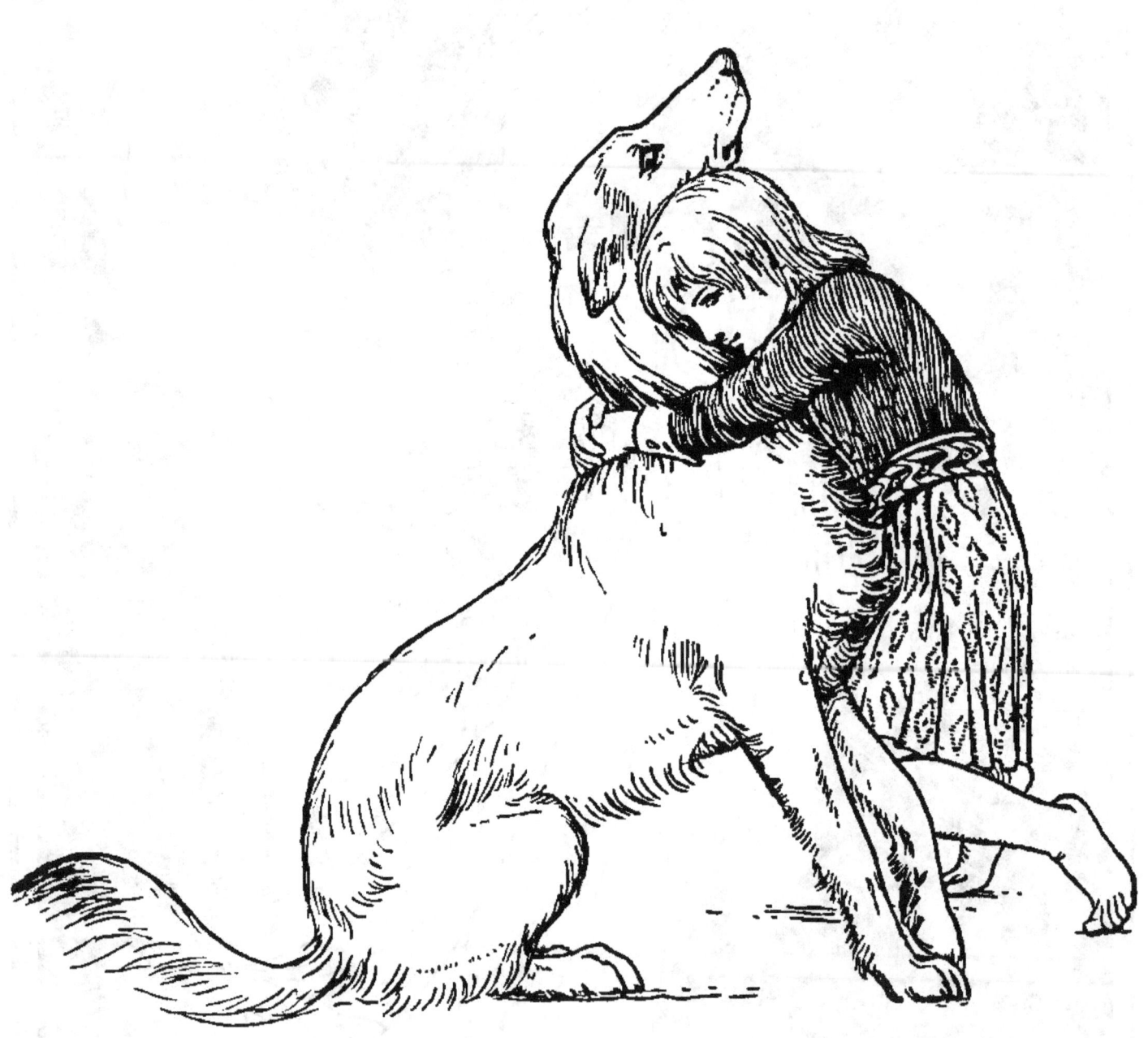

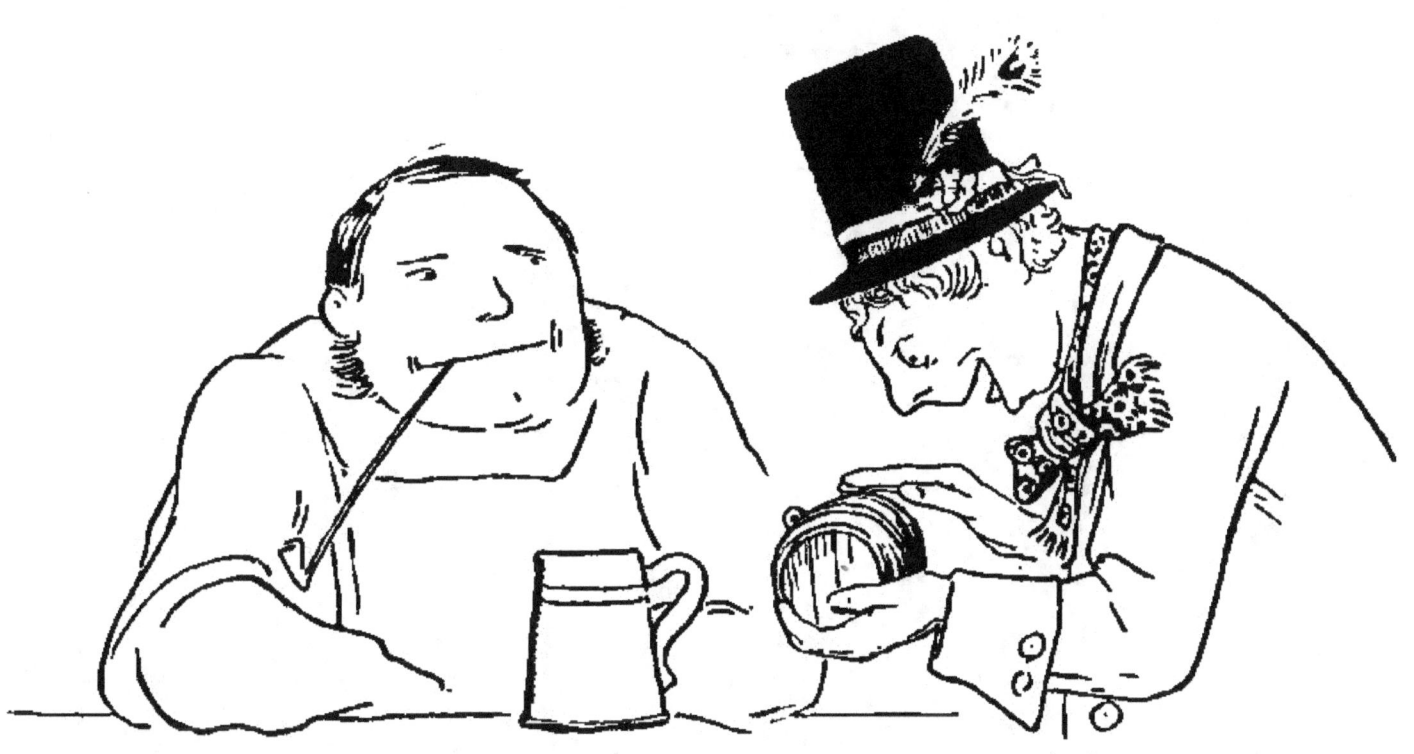

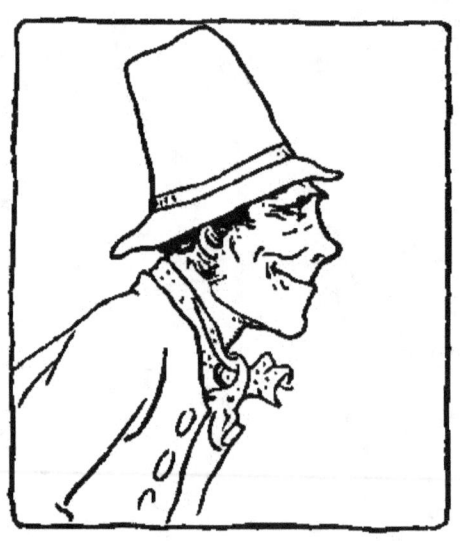

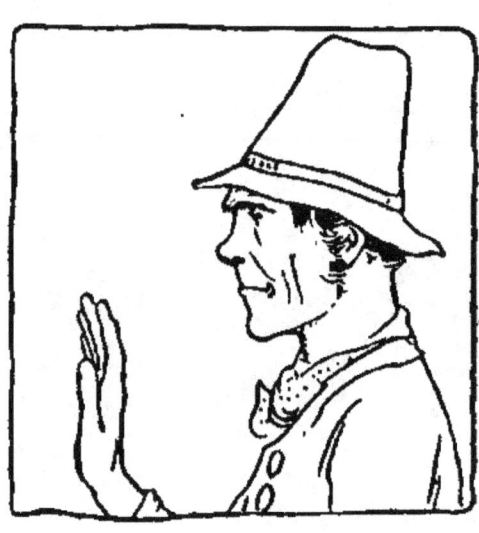

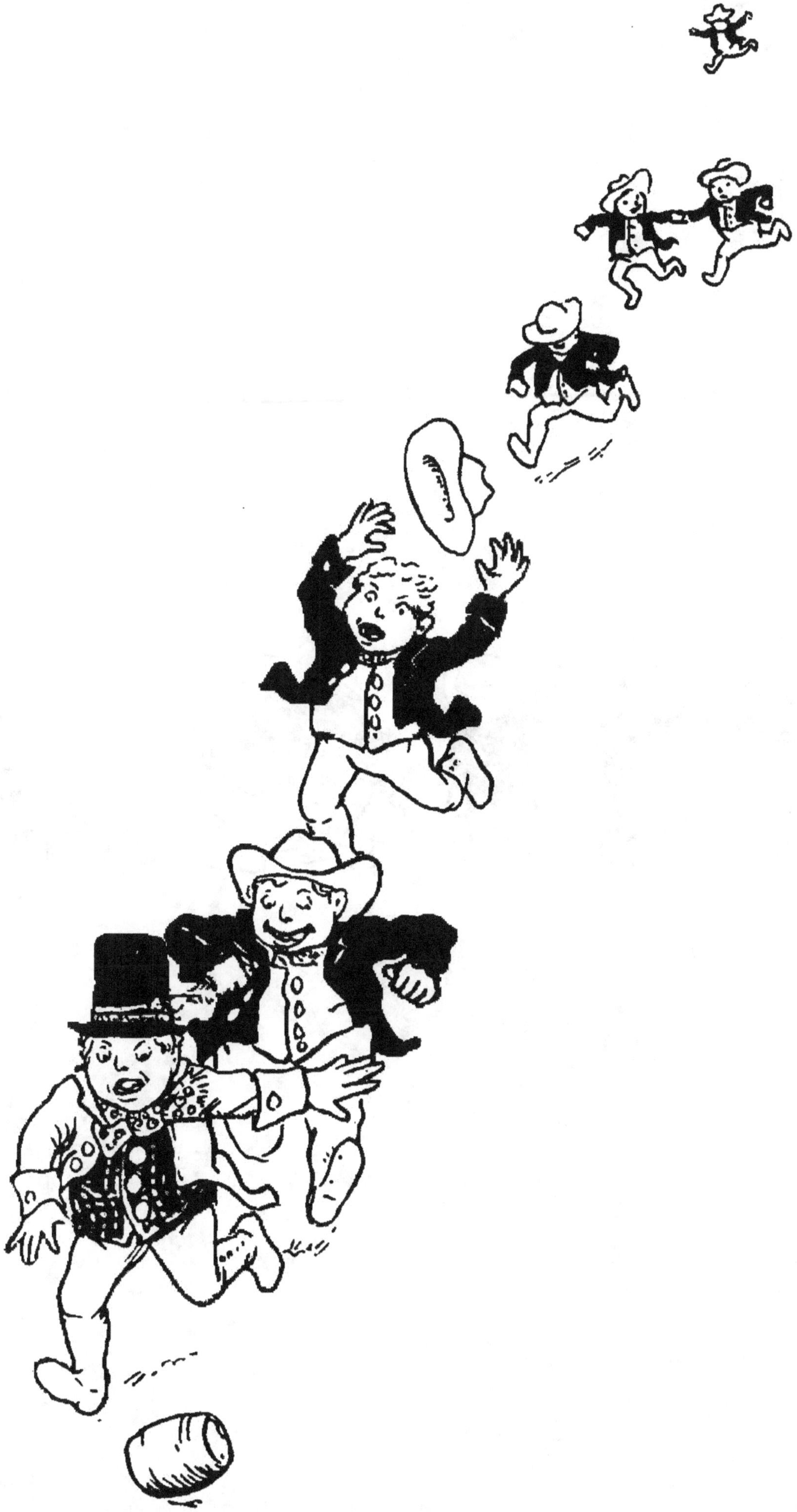

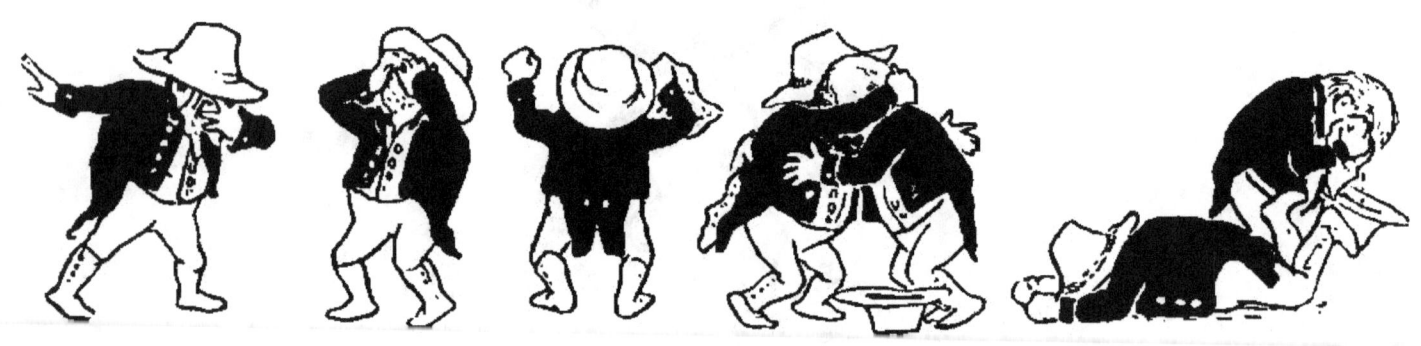

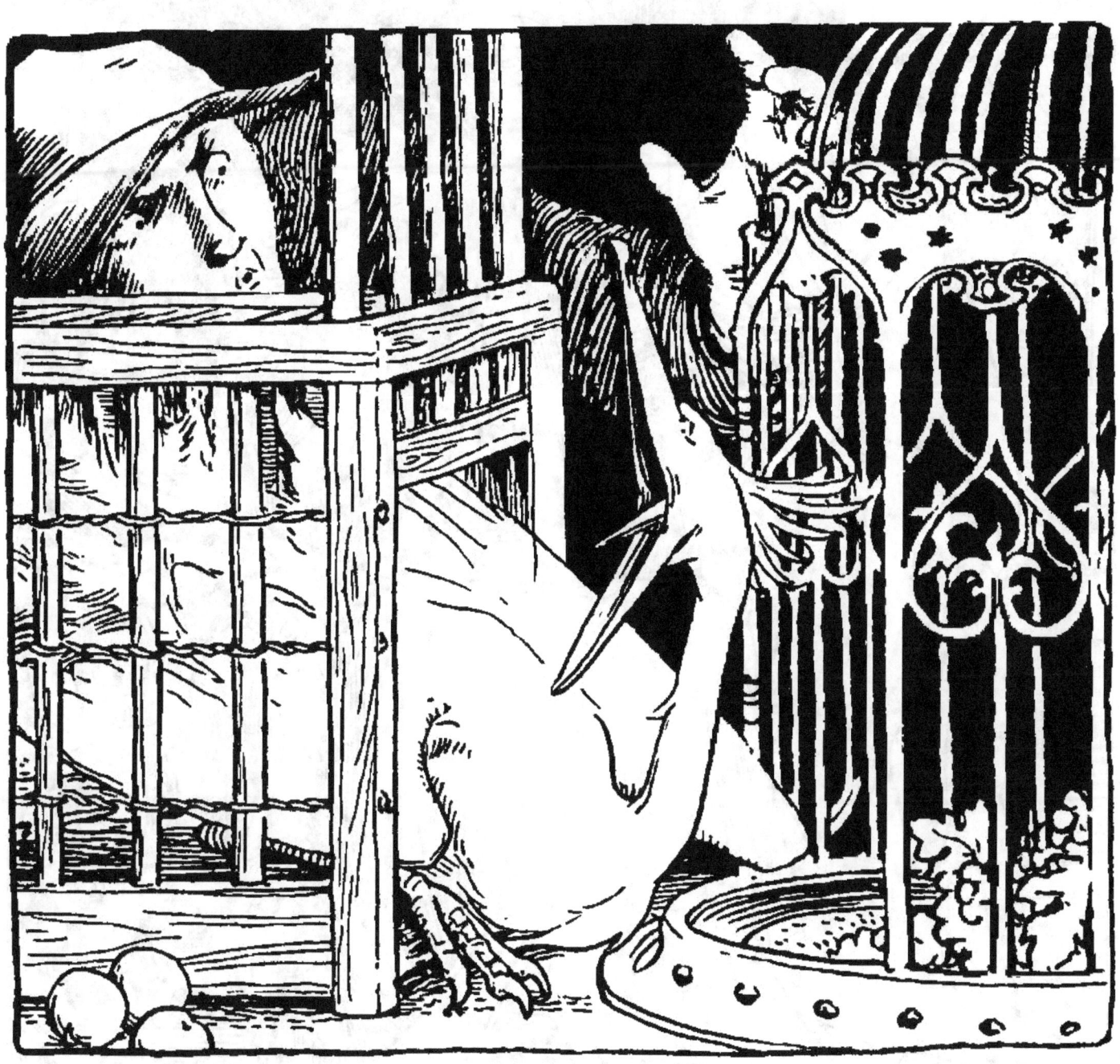

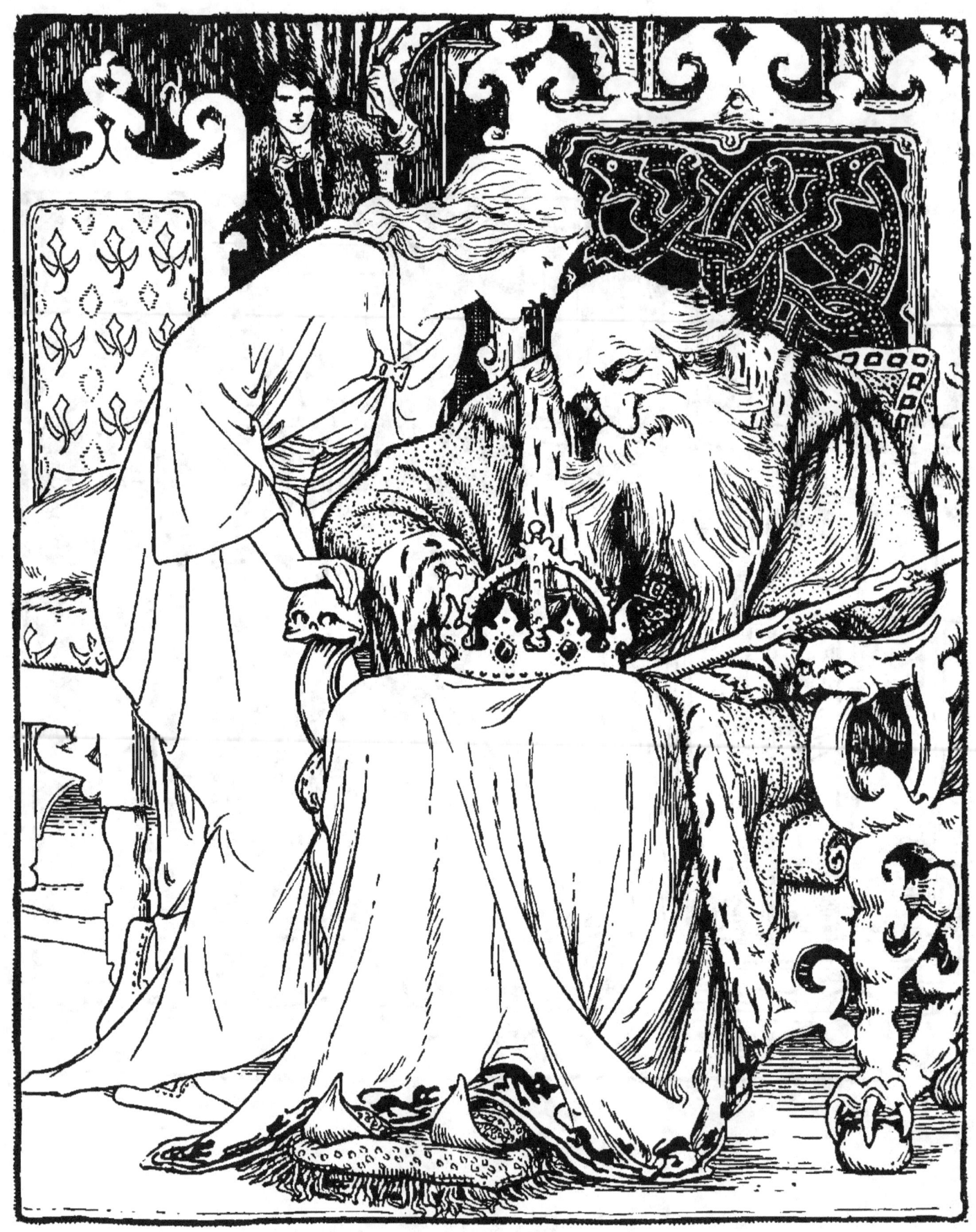

THE GREEK PRINCESS

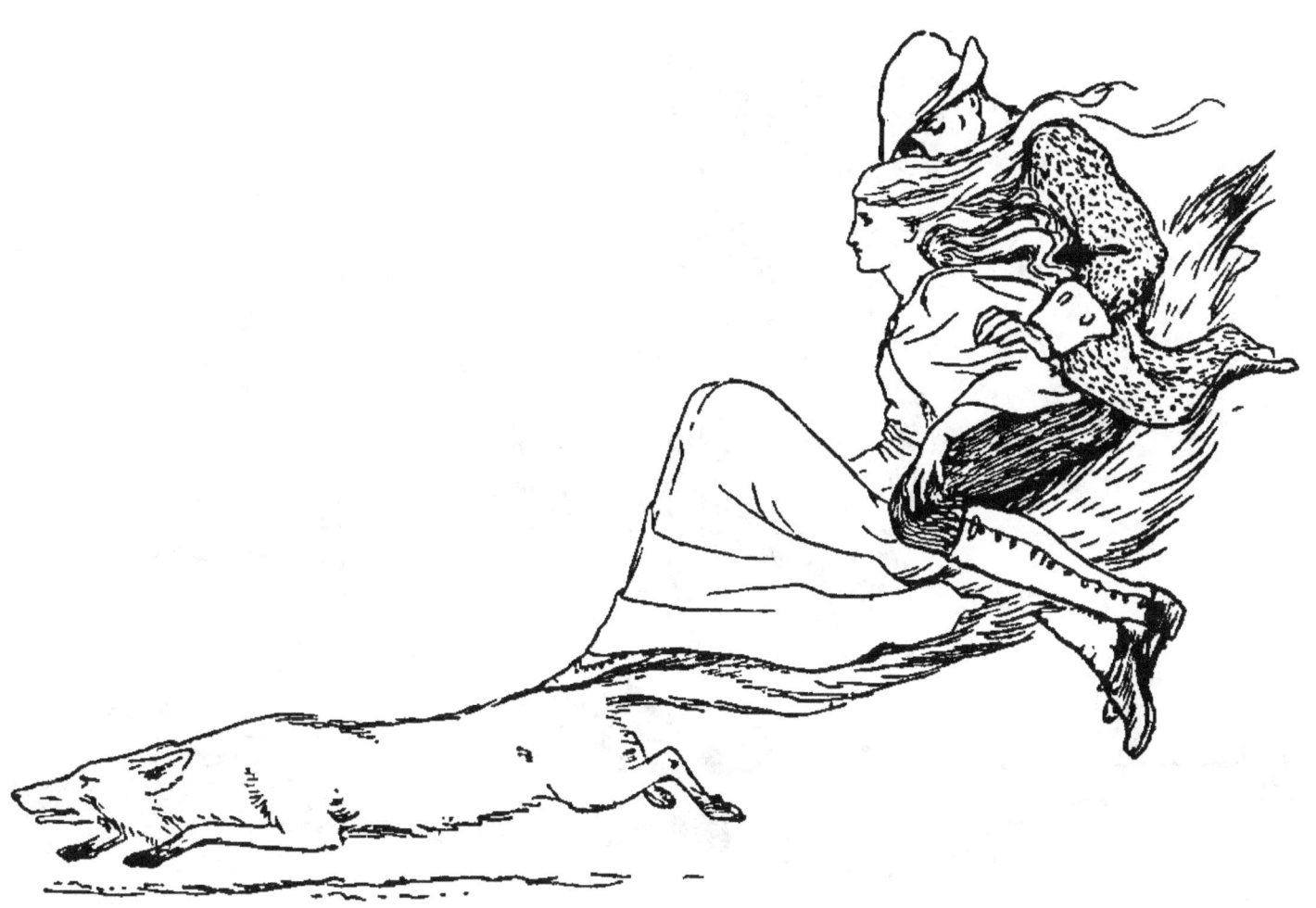

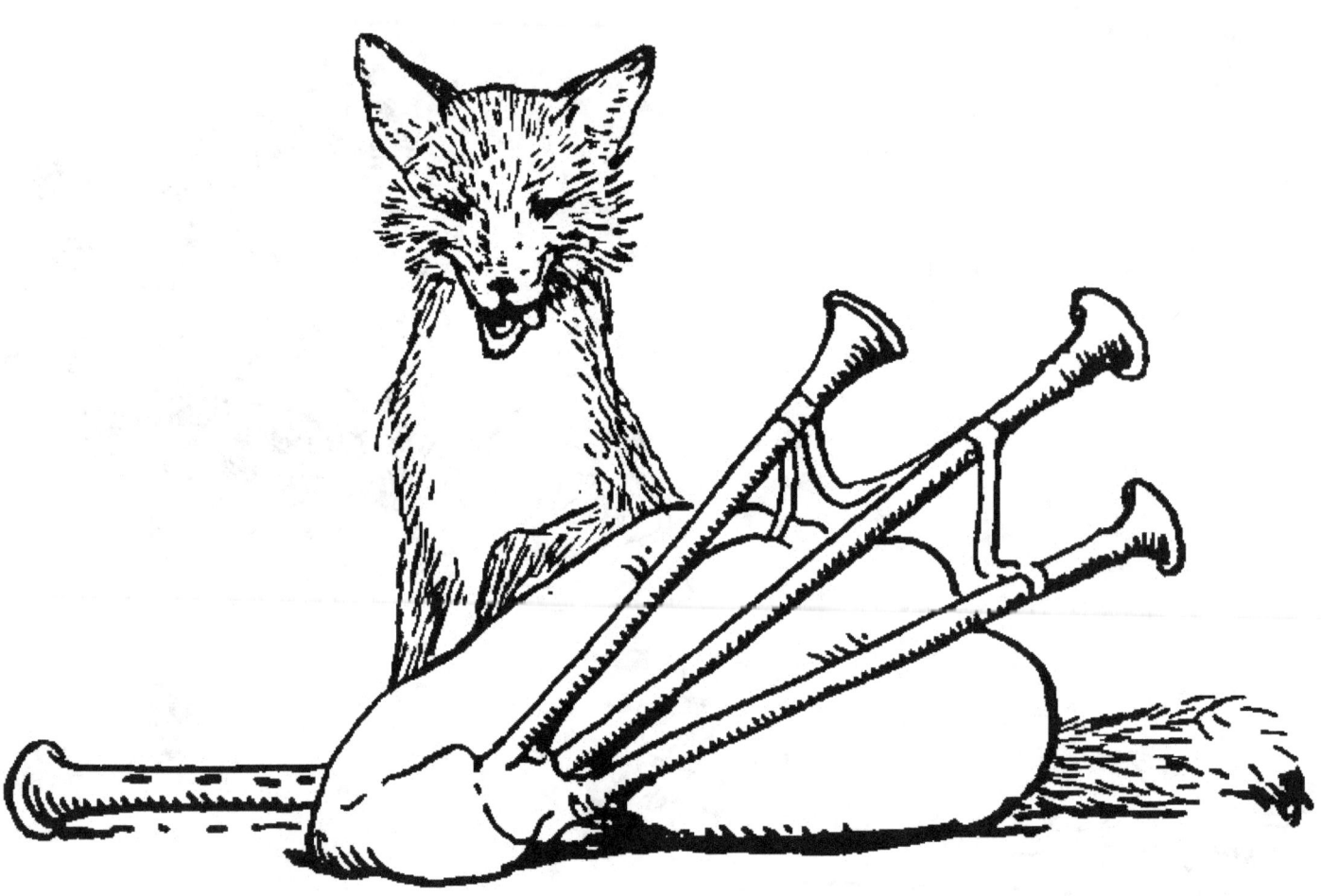

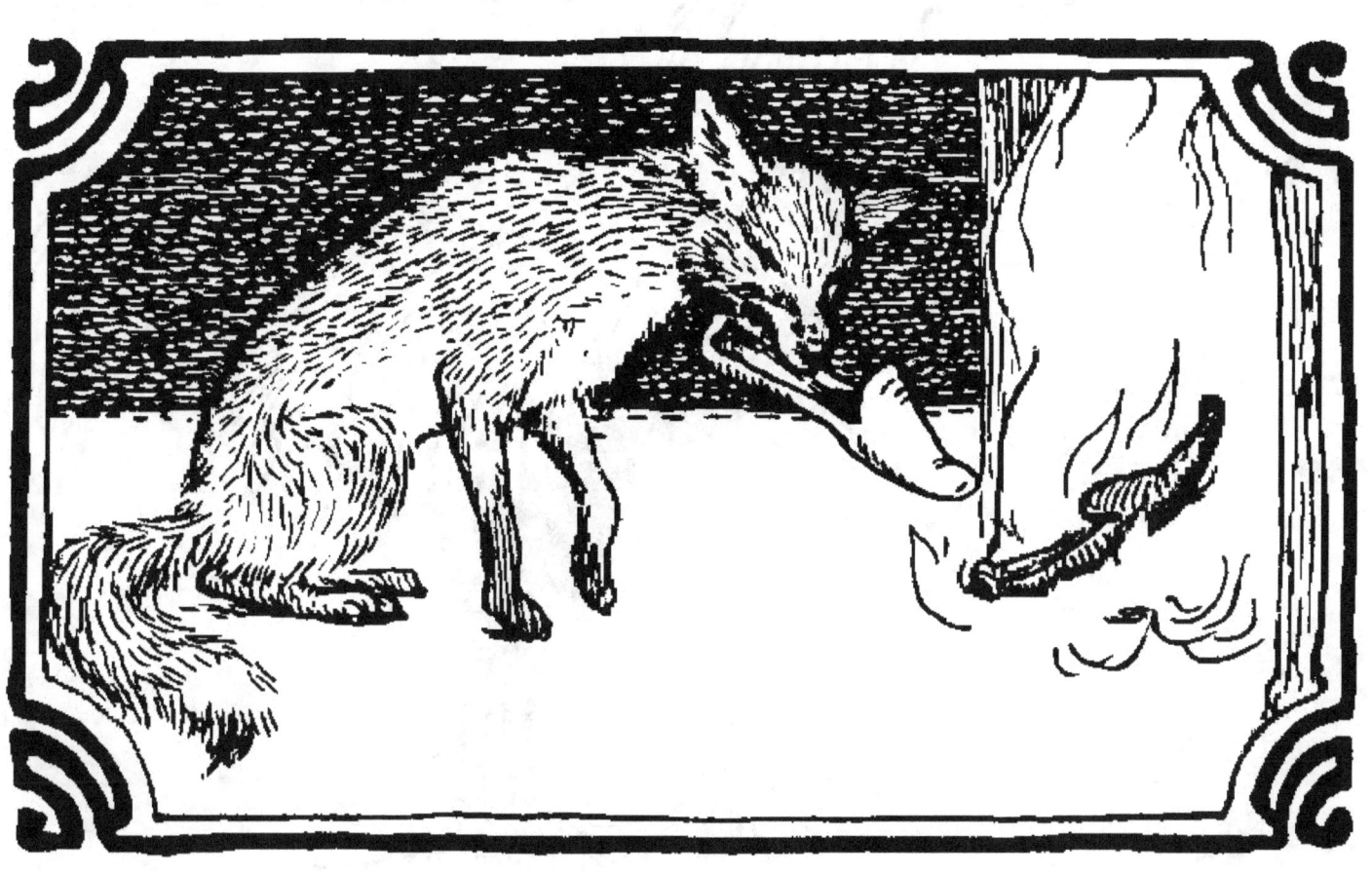

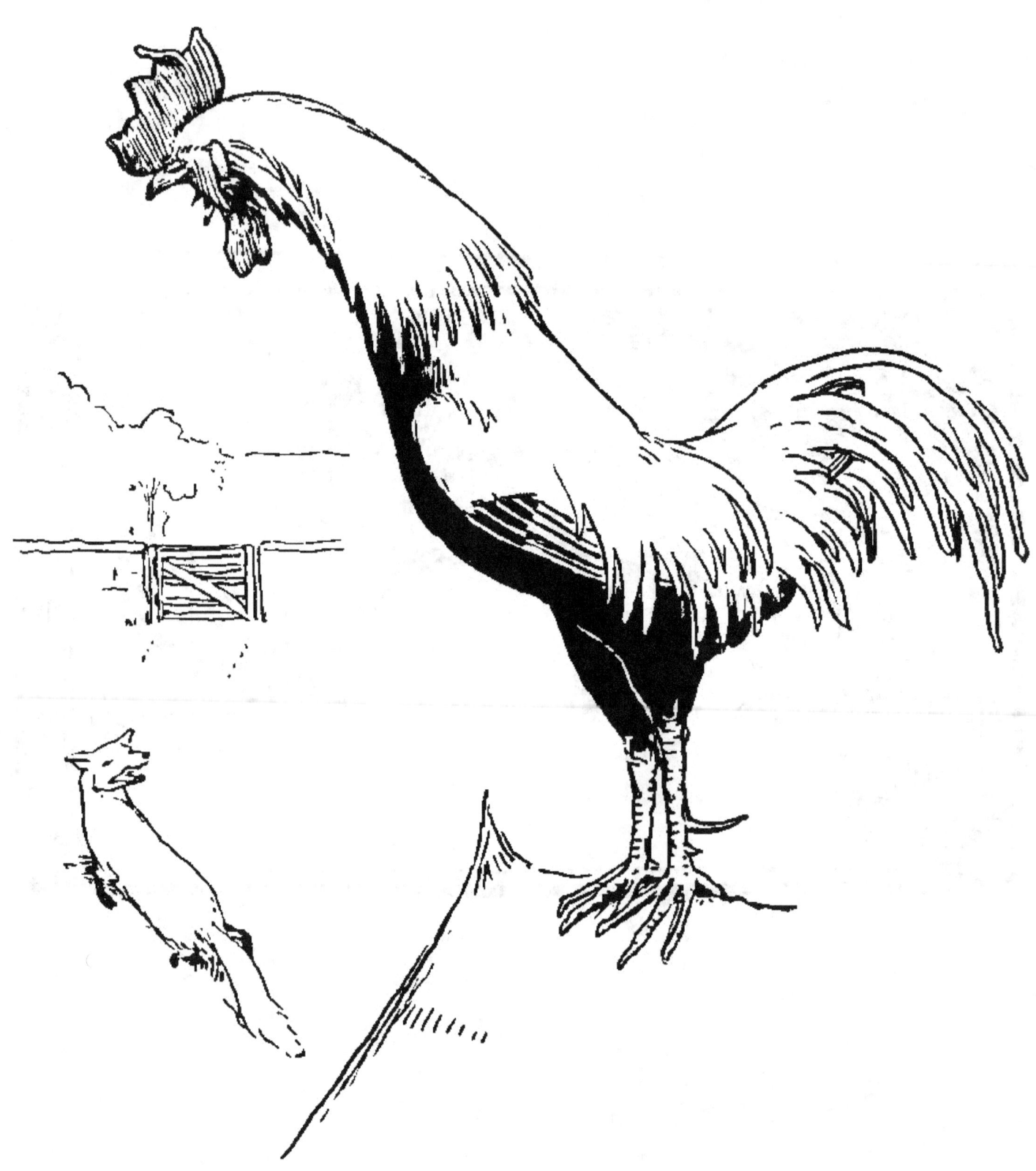

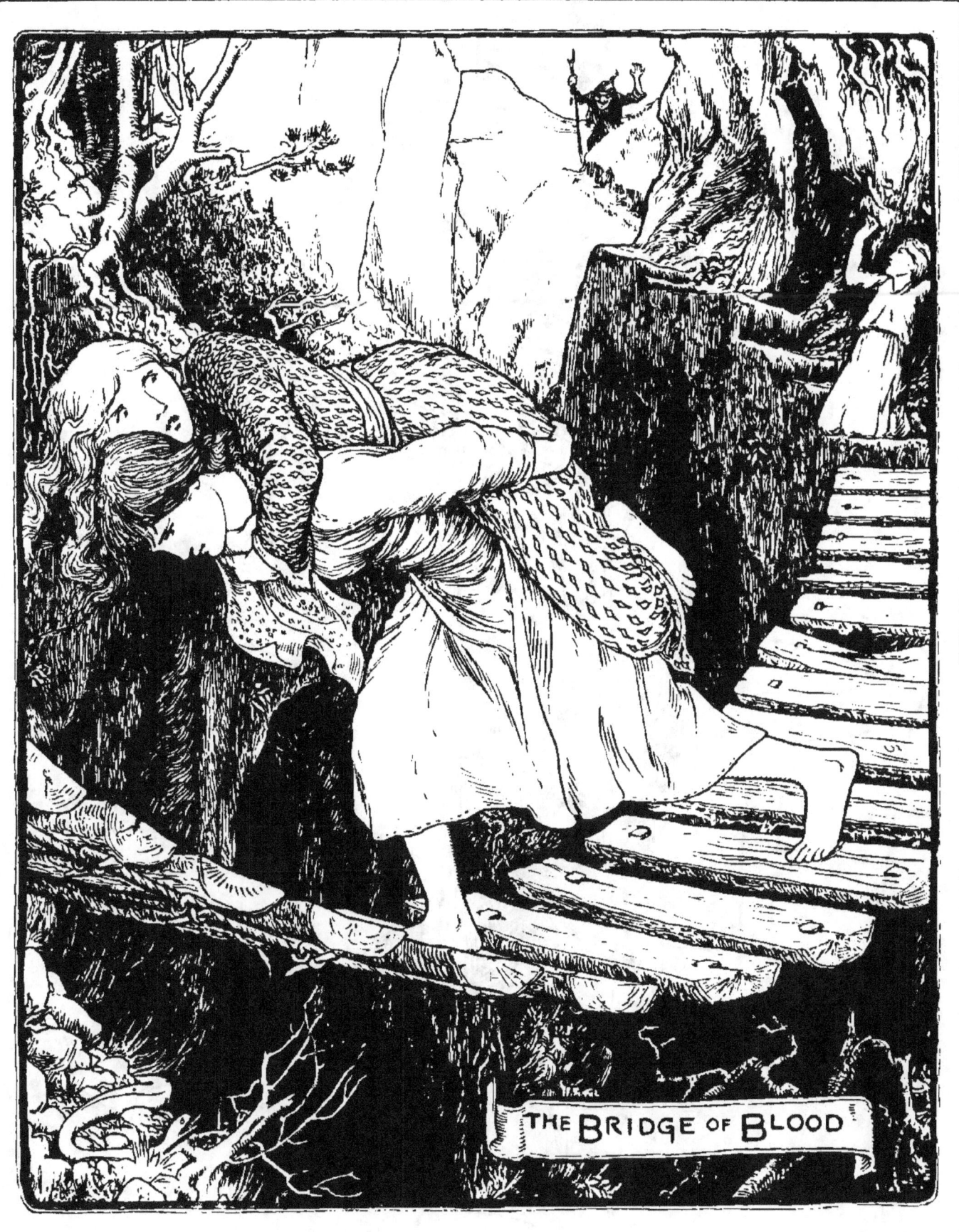

THE BRIDGE OF BLOOD

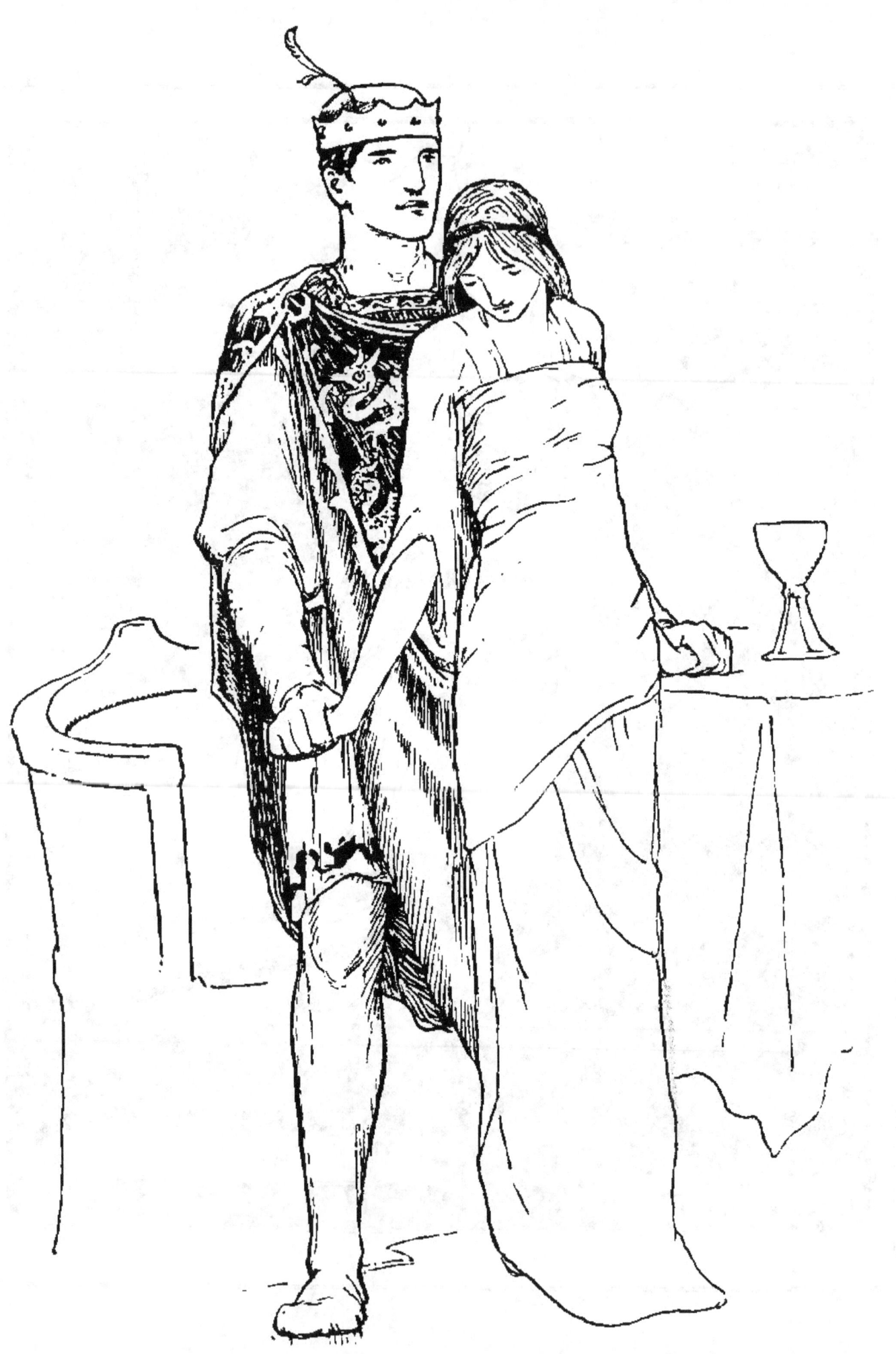

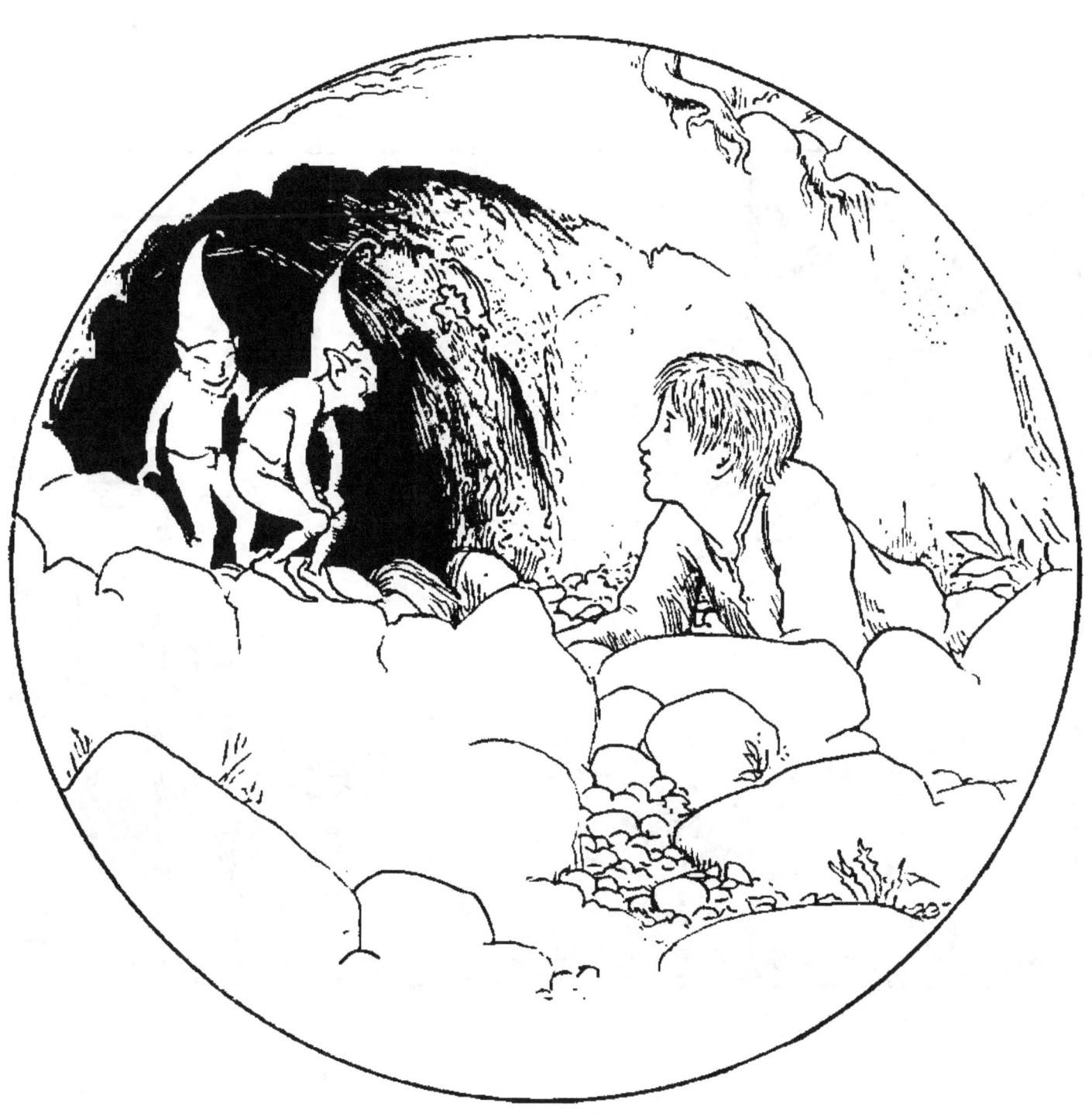

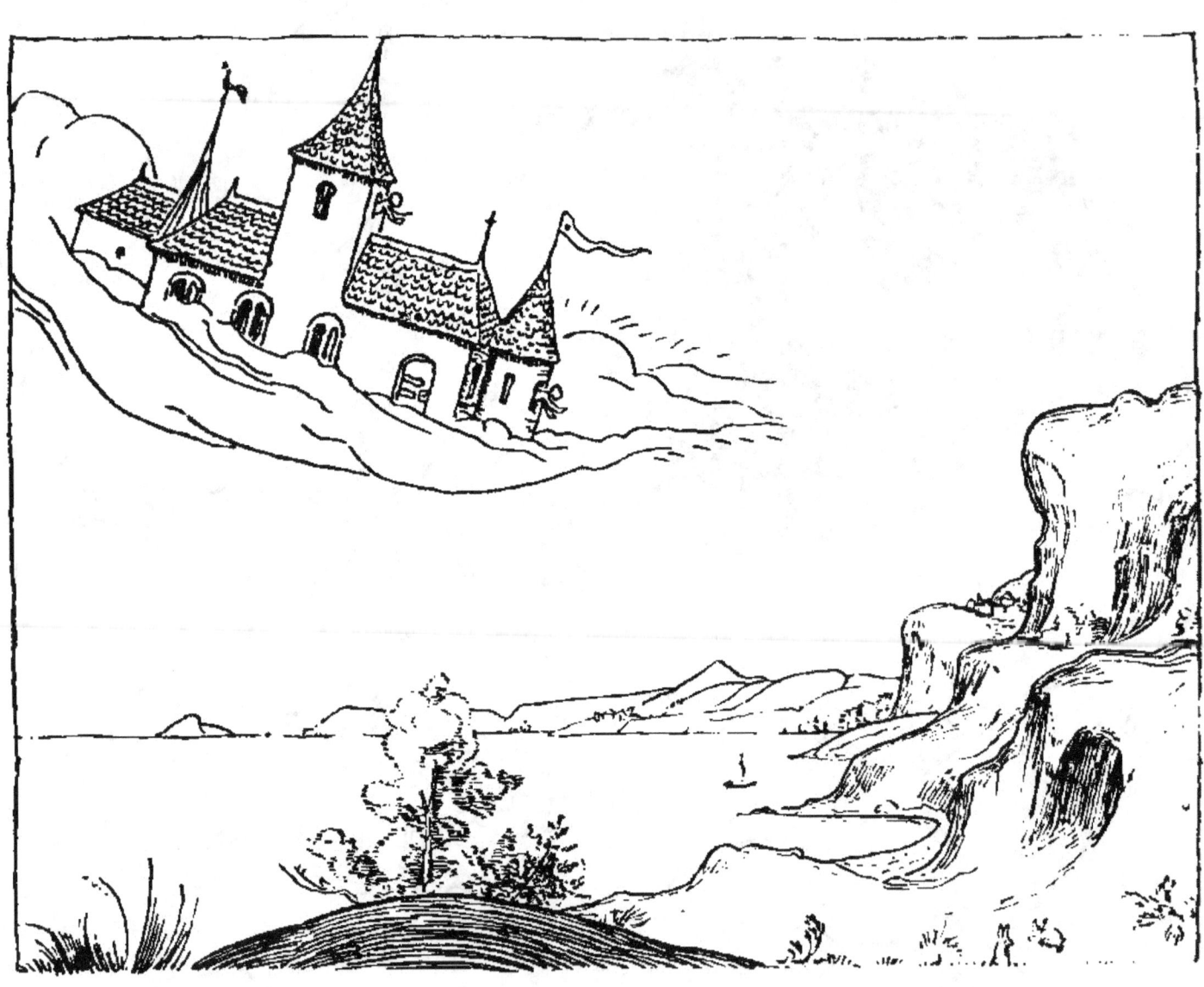

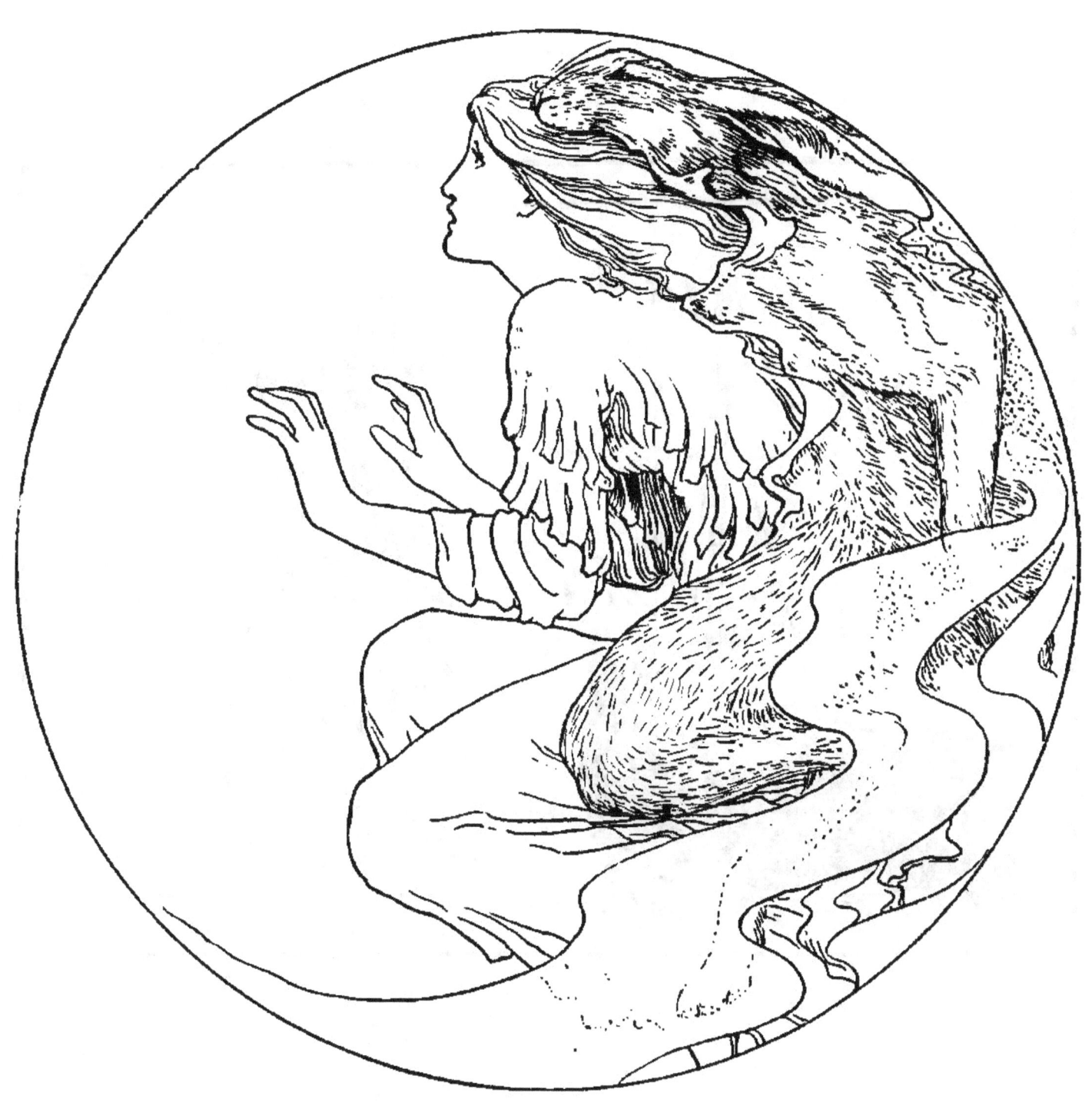

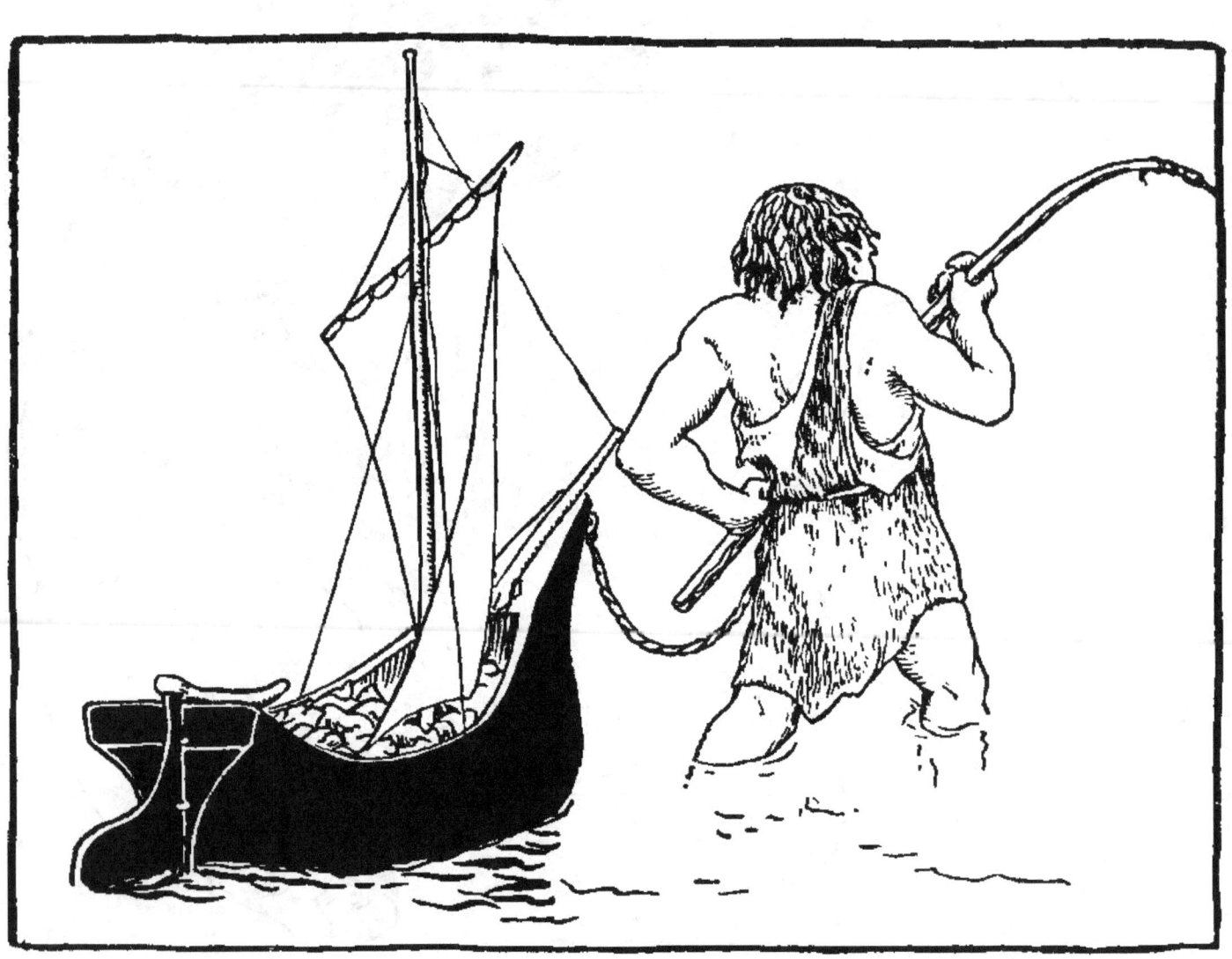

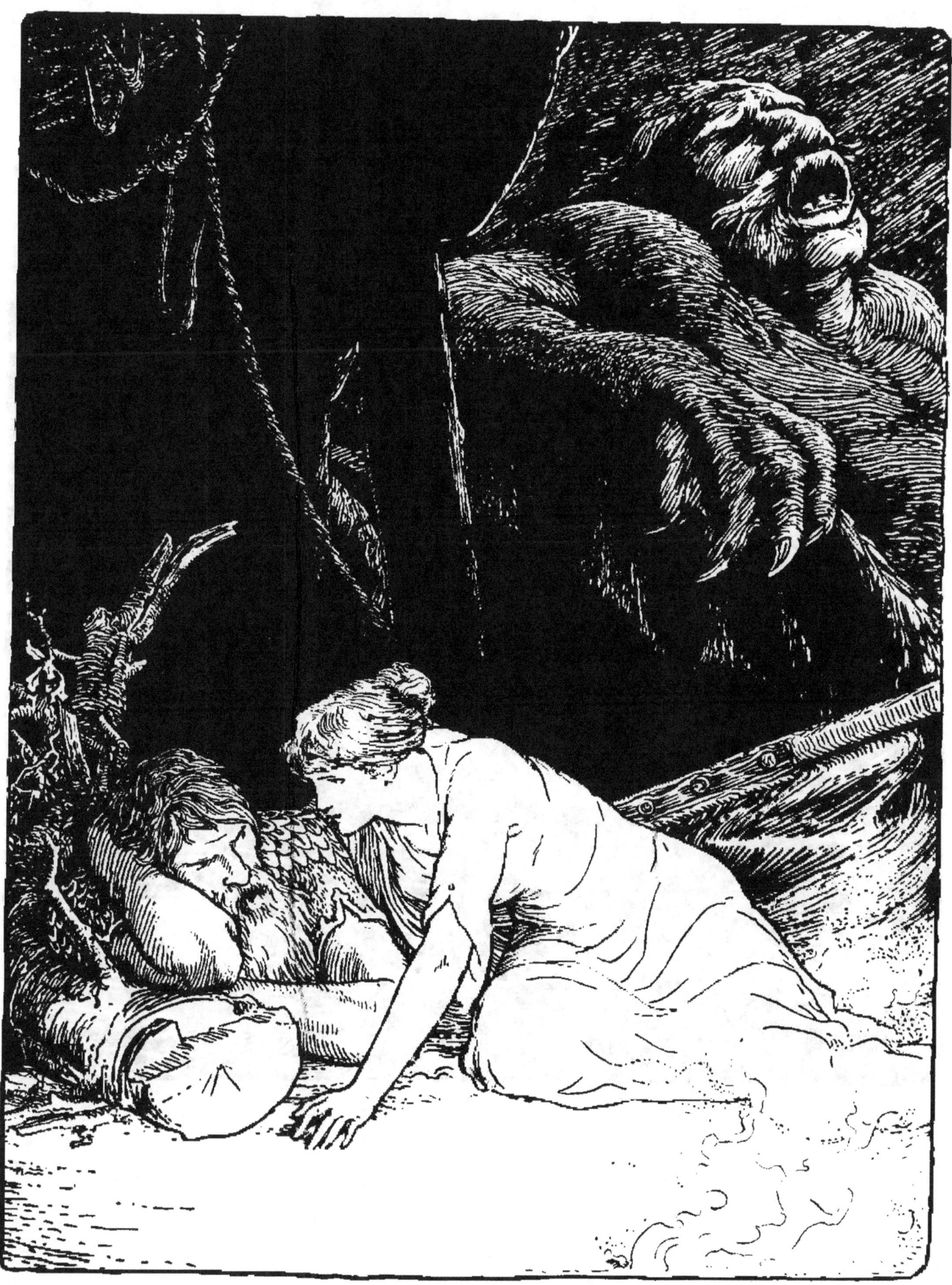

KOISHA KAYN

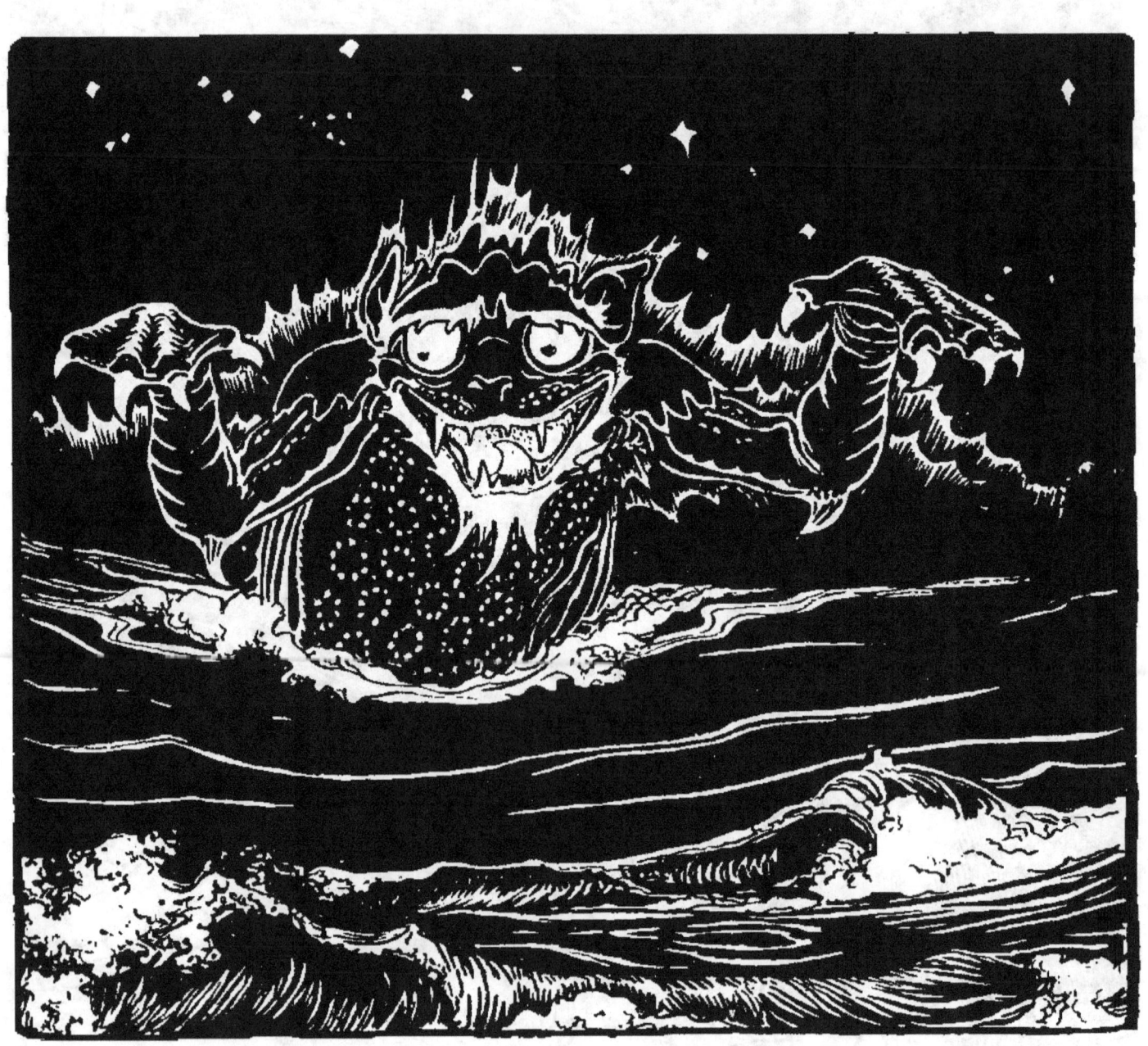

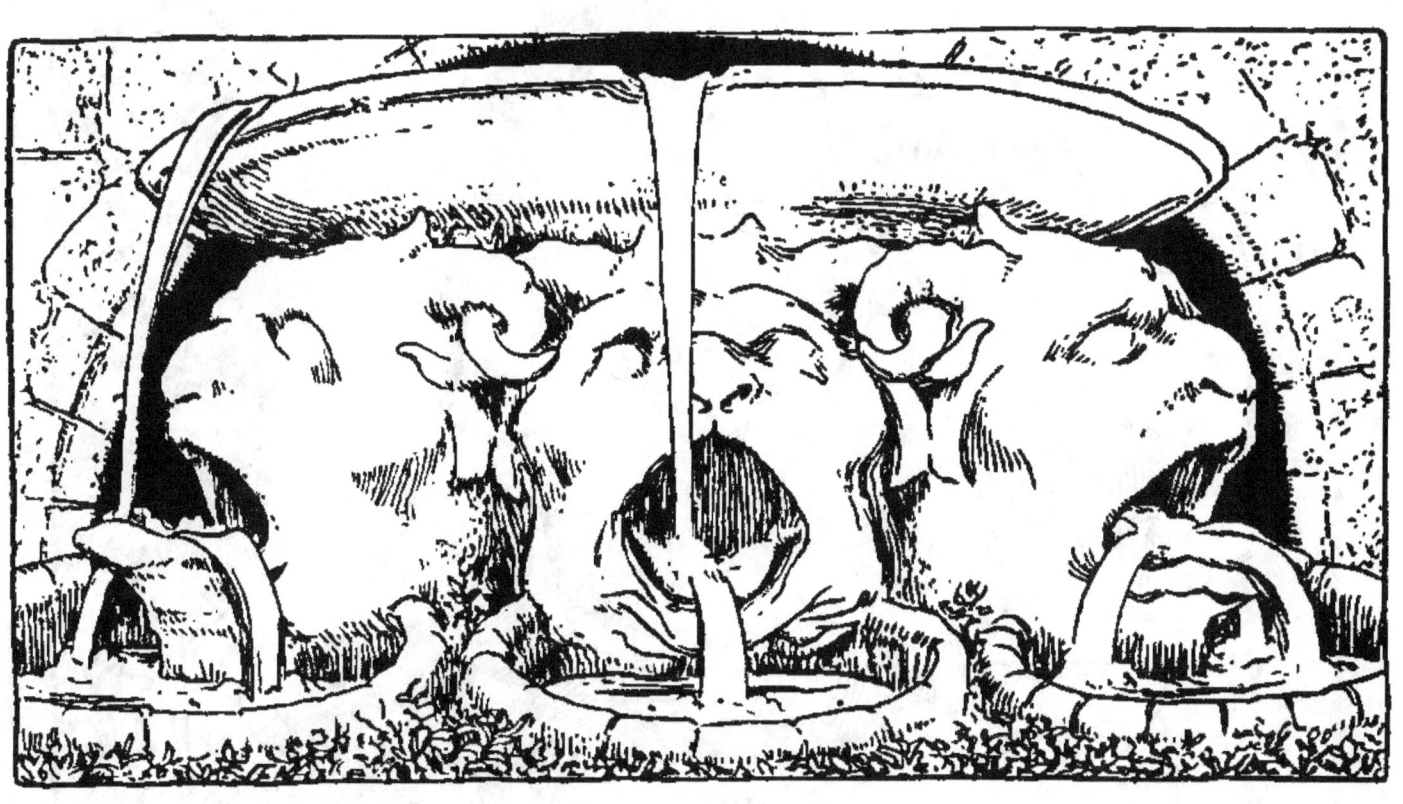

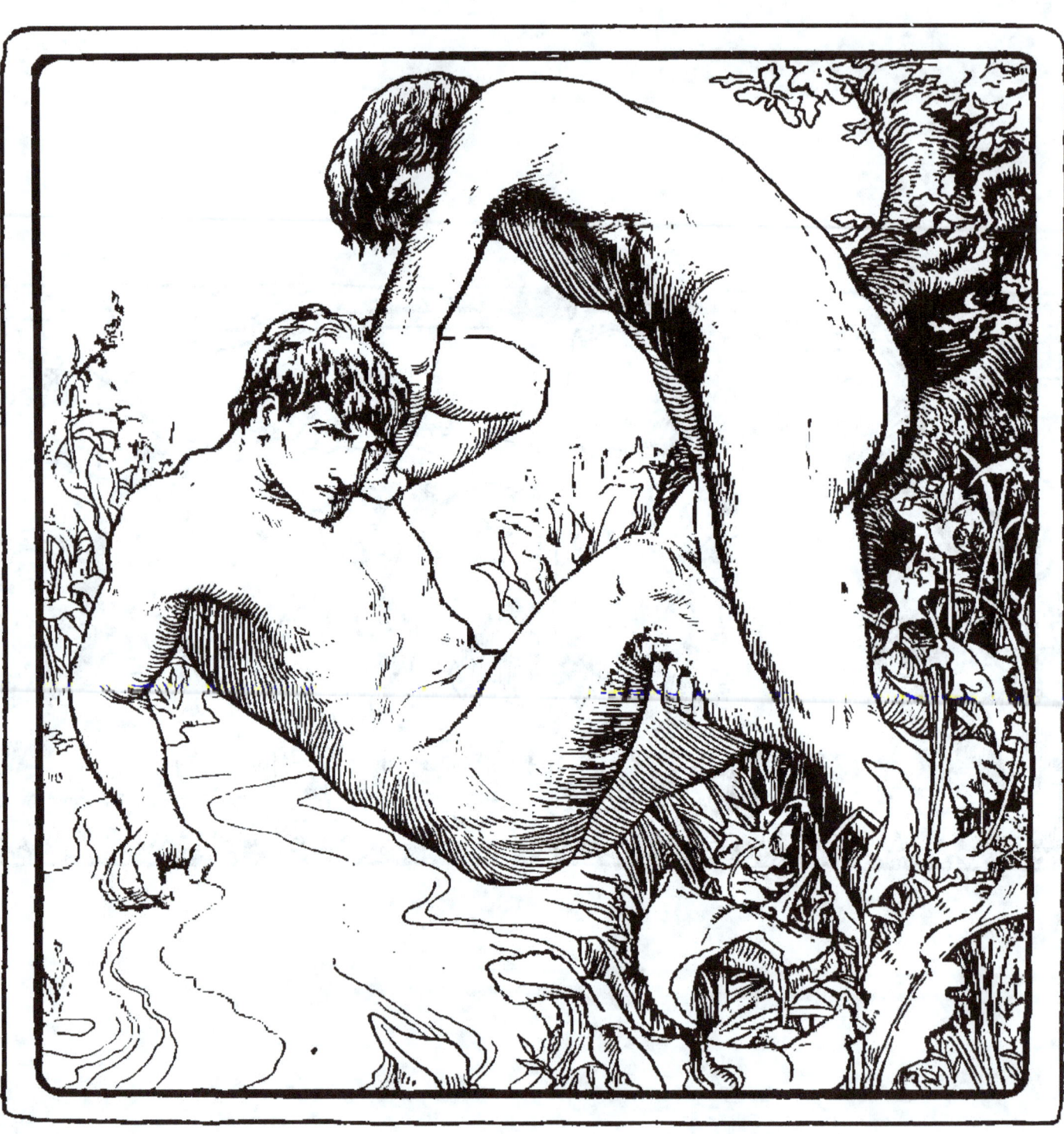

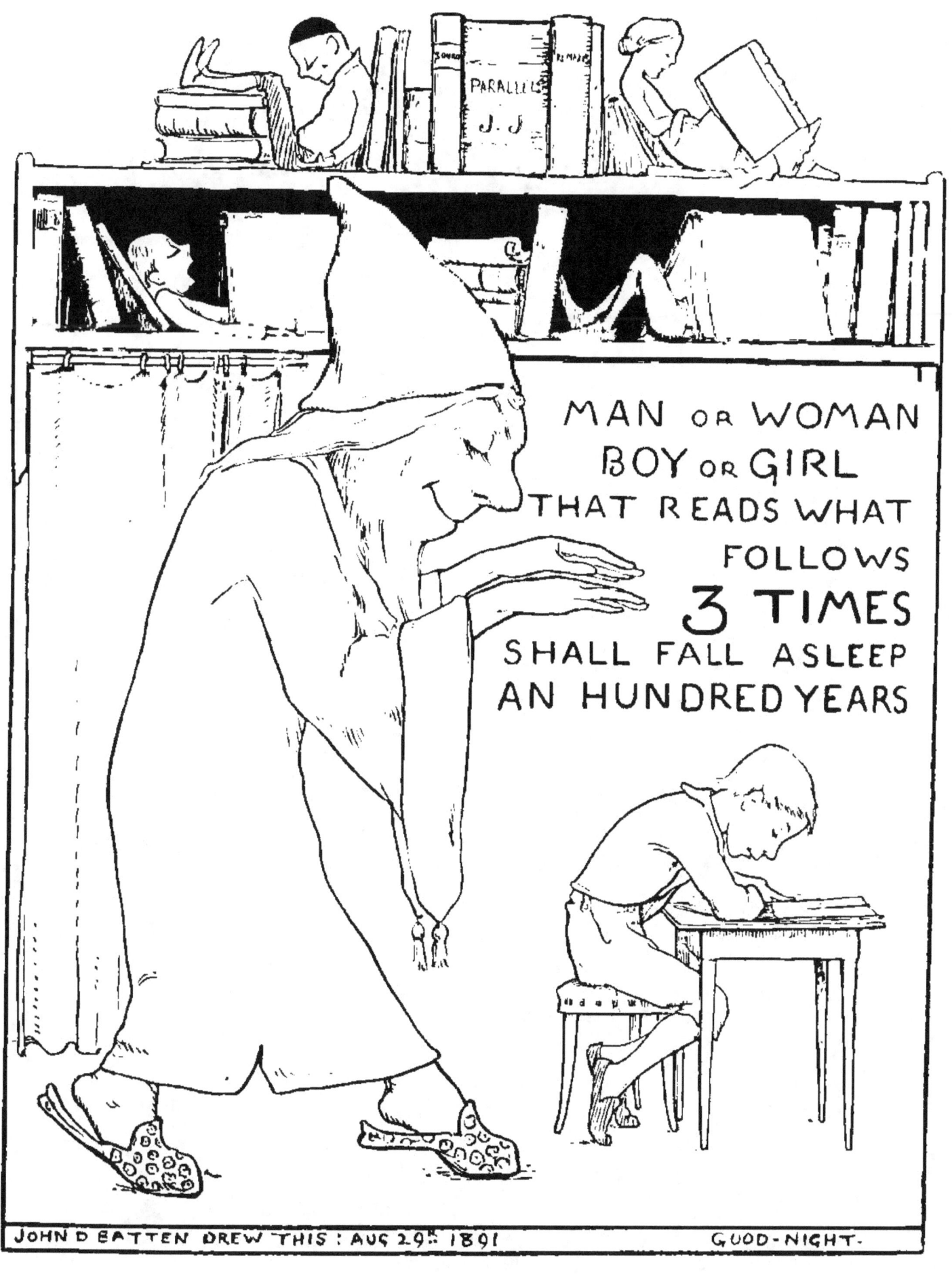

MAN OR WOMAN
BOY OR GIRL
THAT READS WHAT
FOLLOWS
3 TIMES
SHALL FALL ASLEEP
AN HUNDRED YEARS

JOHN D BATTEN DREW THIS : AUG 29TH 1891   GOOD-NIGHT.

www.ingramcontent.com/pod-product-compliance
Lightning Source LLC
Chambersburg PA
CBHW081613220526

45468CB00010B/2860